*Ingrained
Habits*

D1547723

Mary Ellen O'Donnell

# *Ingrained Habits*

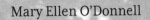

*Growing Up Catholic in*
*Mid-Twentieth-Century*
*America*

*The Catholic University of America Press*
*Washington, D.C.*

Copyright © 2018
The Catholic University of America Press
All rights reserved

The paper used in this publication meets the minimum requirements of
American National Standards for Information Science—Permanence of Paper
for Printed Library Materials, ANSI Z39.48-1984.
∞

Design and composition by Kachergis Book Design

Library of Congress Cataloging-in-Publication Data
Names: O'Donnell, Mary Ellen, author.
Title: Ingrained habits : growing up Catholic in mid-twentieth-century
America / Mary Ellen O'Donnell.
Description: Washington, D.C. : The Catholic University of America Press,
2018. | Includes bibliographical references and index.
Identifiers: LCCN 2017056247 | ISBN 9780813237855 (pbk : alk. paper)
Subjects: LCSH: Catholic Church—United States—History—20th century. |
United States—Religious life and customs.
Classification: LCC BX1406.3 .O36 2018 | DDC 282/.730904—dc23
LC record available at https://lccn.loc.gov/2017056247

*To my parents, Maryanne and Joe Donohue*

# CONTENTS

# ACKNOWLEDGMENTS

This project began over a decade ago in the Department of Religious Studies at the University of North Carolina at Chapel Hill. I am deeply indebted to my teachers and classmates there. I especially want to thank my professors, Laurie Maffly-Kipp, Randall Styers, and Tom Tweed, for their early shepherding of this work, and Ruel Tyson, who impressed on me the art of paying attention to the details. I also want to thank my undergraduate mentors at the University of Scranton, especially Rick Klonoski and Springs Steele. I am grateful for the tireless generosity of Betsey Moylan, whose love of learning and people made her the best research librarian on the planet.

Thank you to Bonnie Oldham for sharing beautiful photographs of St. Madeleine Parish's 1963 May Crowning in Ridley Park, Pennsylvania, which fulfilled my dream for a cover image.

In sixth grade, Sr. Daria taught me how to diagram a sentence, and this instilled a lifelong appreciation for the challenge and reward of well-structured language on the page. I am ever grateful for those lessons.

My fellow St. Paul School alums helped jog my memory about our shared formative days there. Thank you to Mandi Boyanoski, Chrissy

Haggerty, Mari LaVigna, and Kristy Voytek for traveling down memory lane with me and encouraging me on every step. Thank you also to Becky Kelly, Bridget Kettel, and Alison Skoff for their friendship throughout the process. My aunt Ellen O'Brien read an early draft of this work at a pivotal time for me and offered not only insightful feedback on my writing, but also rich memories of my mother's family that reminded me why I was doing this in the first place.

I am grateful for the conversation partners I was lucky to find in colleagues and students at Mercyhurst University and Chestnut Hill College. I also want to thank many friends and fellow parents whose interest in my writing, inquired about at playgrounds, parties, and school functions, consistently motivated me to get back to it. My sincerest appreciation goes to so many family members for their love and support of all things I do, this writing thing among them.

I want to thank Mary Gordon for her collection of work. On a personal level, I want to express my gratitude to her for taking an interest in my research and inviting me into her life for a day, as well as for enduring a harrowing flight out of Erie, Pennsylvania, only because she had accepted my invitation to speak there. I cannot resist the opportunity to thank her publicly.

I am grateful to the Catholic University of America Press, particularly to Trevor Lipscombe, who, with wit and wisdom, patiently guided me through this process. This book would not exist if Trevor had not given me the nudge I needed at just the right time, unbeknownst to him, as I was mourning the death of my mother and celebrating the birth of my second child. His direction and his feedback on drafts improved my work at every turn. I am also indebted to my anonymous reviewers, whose critiques and suggestions pushed the manuscript where it needed to go. It is a much better book because of their careful and generous readings. Thank you to Aldene Fredenburg for her copyediting during the final stages of publication.

We cannot choose our siblings, but given the chance, I would choose mine. My brothers, Joe and Patrick Donohue, indulged much talk of our Catholic grade-school years, and I am ever grateful for their love and support. My sister, Ann Martin, engaged not only my reminiscing but also my early drafts and ongoing gripes about the challenge of the writing process, always with understanding, encouragement, and lots of love.

Three people have witnessed up close the transformation of this project from its beginnings in Chapel Hill to what follows on these pages. They ensured my survival during graduate school and have buoyed me in life, both professionally and personally, since then. Shanny Luft and Chad Seales read drafts, asked questions, and pushed my thinking; their relentless encouragement of and convincing interest in my work helped get me here. Kathryn Lofton did the impossible by creating time. It is the only way I can make sense of her ability to respond to the countless emails I sent with ideas, doubts, or pages. She always said the right thing, even when it was not what I wanted to hear, and she did it with loving attention and unconditional support.

I want to thank my daughter, Clare, for taking an interest in my work with a wisdom beyond her years, never missing an opportunity to share her pride with anyone who would listen, and giving me every reason to persist at writing. I want to thank my son, Daniel, for confirming that joy and love can be incarnate and for sharing both. I am grateful to them for making all things matter in new ways. The commitment of my husband, Michael, to this project emerges in every chapter. Always game for talking through an idea or editing pages, he brings a thoughtful perspective and careful eye that invariably improve my work. Only because of his steady presence, loving humor, and firm encouragement, as we both buried parents and changed diapers, was I able to write this book.

This book is dedicated to my parents, Maryanne and Joe Donohue. My mother may not have lived to see me publish the book, but her fingerprints are all over my writing as my first and best editor. My father picked up the slack with a belief in the project and a level of support never to be matched. Their faith in God and their faith in us somehow make the world go 'round.

# PREFACE

Explaining to my then three-year-old daughter why my husband, she, and I were going to church on a chilly November Saturday morning proved an unexpected challenge.

"We are going to remember Grandma at God's house."

"Is Grandma going to be there?"

"No, you remember that Grandma died and is in Heaven. Today the people at church are going to remember her in a special way."

"But I thought you said Grandma was with God and we were going to God's house."

Right. As many times as I had explained religious and theological concepts to rooms full of college students, I had been failing pretty miserably with my own daughter. Fortunately, the questions quickly ceased when she saw that my sister and brother-in-law were two of the remarkably few people inside the church. Nearly all the adults in the pews looked more like her grandmother, an observation that held the potential for even more confusion were it not for the thrilling distraction of her aunt and uncle's presence. Her attendance, and volume, certainly surprised the regulars at this daily Mass. I spent most of the thirty-five minutes trying to keep her occupied and answer her questions as efficiently and satisfactorily as possible. My husband, sister, brother-in-law, and I all agreed that my mother would have loved her energy and inquisitiveness, so it seemed a fitting way to spend a Mass said in my mother's name. My father had already been to countless of these masses—those dedicated by thoughtful parishioners who donated money to the church to have Mass said in her memory—since my mother's death only a few months earlier. He certainly would have joined us had it not been the fiftieth anniversary of his own father's untimely passing. He was a few miles across town at a different church, where Mass was similarly being said in his father's memory.

My own failures at my daughter's religious formation notwithstanding, the jarring contrast between her youthful naiveté and the steady prayer of the elderly regulars stood as a poignant example of the generational chasm emerging in American Catholic experience. Indeed, her introduction to this religious tradition would differ strikingly from that of her grandmother, whose memory and faith were being honored in this church, and from that of her grandfather, who was worshiping down the road in the parish in which he was raised. Suddenly it felt surreal that something that had so significantly shaped my parents' identities could seem so foreign to my child at this point. This was not a question of faith in God or even a reflection on my own catechetical oversights up to that point. This was about a fundamental difference in the way that Catholicism has been lived, shared, and internalized in the United States across these recent generations.

The Second Vatican Council, convened by Pope John XXIII in 1962 and continuing beyond his death to 1965, drastically altered Catholic life around the world. The church was already in the process of changing, but for the faithful in the pews the Council's documents affected everything, from details of worship to metaphors for the church. As transformations prescribed in the document entitled *Constitution on the Sacred Liturgy* were eventually implemented into practice throughout the following decade, no longer would these people observe a priest saying Mass in Latin for the devoted believers in the Church Militant; they could now participate in Mass in their own language as equal members of the People of God. Further, in life outside the church in the United States, the election of a Catholic president in 1960, along with Catholic migration from secluded city neighborhoods to the expanding suburbs, indicated that Catholics would no longer remain on the margins of American life. Catholicism was changing with dramatic shifts in theology and demographics. As church members were adjusting to new ritual forms and neighborhood circumstances, they were also adapting to an ecumenical openness to other faiths and to new doubts about God's wrathful judgment. This study is not in these large developments but rather in the subtler sphere of intimate encounters before, or while, these developments were happening.

In the past few decades, significant scholarly attention has been devoted to the history of Catholics in the United States, with some works tracing ecclesiological developments and others intentionally focusing beyond the church's institutional constructs. Texts such as Patrick Carey's *Catholics in America: A History* and others, like *American Catholics in Transition*, by William D'Antonio, Michelle Dillon, and Mary L. Gautier, provide a window onto a dynamic, changing community.[1] There has also been much journalistic consideration of distinct generations of Catholics currently living in the United States and their relative levels of identification with and adherence to their faith.[2] The debate about what constitutes a "Catholic iden-

1. Patrick Carey, *Catholics in America: A History* (Lanham, Md.: Rowman and Littlefield, 2008); William D'Antonio, Michelle Dillon, and Mary L. Gautier, *American Catholics in Transition* (Lanham, Md.: Rowman and Littlefield, 2013).

2. For examples, see the series "Catholics in America," *National Catholic Reporter*, October 24, 2011, https://www.ncronline.org/AmericanCatholics?_ga=1.265451149.321788764.1461956502, accessed July 18, 2016; William D'Antonio, James Davidson, Mary Gautier, and Katherine Meyer, "Assumptions in Study on Young Catholics Lead to Unnecessarily Grim Outlook," *National Catholic Reporter*, December 6, 2014, https://www.ncronline.org/

tity" has filled countless pages and has ranged from concern over university curricula to disputes over Eucharistic participation.[3] Clearly what it means to be, or have been, Catholic in this country demands careful investigation from a multitude of perspectives. The United States has created a challenging situation for American Catholics to navigate. The country's relative youth, rebellion against a distant seat of authority, complicated Protestant Christian history, and political ideologies have created a bumpy road for Catholicism's development here. As the historical and sociological literature of American Catholicism continues to expand, it calls for a closer look at the more personal encounters. I want to examine

---

news/people/assumptions-study-young-catholics-lead-unnessarily-grim-outlook, accessed July 19, 2016; Elizabeth Flock, "Generation X Becoming Less Catholic and Less Republican," *U.S. News and World Report*, May 31, 2012, http://www.usnews.com/news/articles/2012/05/31/generation-x-becoming-less-catholic-and-less-republican-, accessed July 19, 2016; Mark M. Gray, "Your Average American Catholic," *America: National Catholic Review*, May 18, 2015, http://americamagazine.org/issue/your-average-american-catholic, accessed July 19, 2016; Michael Paulson, "Even as Hispanics Lift Catholicism, Many Are Leaving the Church," *New York Times*, May 7, 2014, http://www.nytimes.com/2014/05/08/upshot/even-as-hispanics-lift-catholicism-theyre-leaving-it.html, accessed July 19, 2016.

3. For examples, see George W. Traub, ed., *A Jesuit Education Reader* (Chicago: Loyola Press, 2008); John R. Wilcox and Irene King, eds., *Enhancing Religious Identity: Best Practices from Catholic Campuses* (Washington, D.C.: Georgetown University Press, 2000); Charlotte Hayes, "Catholic Identity and the Core Curriculum at Notre Dame," *National Catholic Register*, January 1, 2015, http://www.ncregister.com/daily-news/catholic-identity-and-the-core-curriculum-at-notre-dame/, accessed July 19, 2016; Jim McDermott, "It's Commencement Controversy Season!," *America: National Catholic Review*, May 5, 2016, http://americamagazine.org/content/dispatches/its-commencement-controversy-season, accessed January 19, 2016; Valerie Schmalz, "University President Defends Hiring for Catholic Identity," *American Catholic*, July 13, 2016, http://www.americancatholic.org/news/report.aspx?id=44844, accessed July 19, 2016; Michael S. Rosenwald and Michelle Boorstein, "Denying Communion: A Priest and a Lesbian Set Off a Catholic Culture Clash," *Washington Post*, March 17, 2012, https://www.washingtonpost.com/local/denying-communion-a-priest-and-a-lesbian-set-off-a-catholic-culture-clash/2012/03/15/gIQA9roNJS_story.html, accessed July 19, 2016; Frans Jozef Van Beeck, "Denying Communion to Politicians: A Theologian Explains Why It's Wrong," *Commonweal*, June 14, 2004, https://www.commonwealmagazine.org/denying-communion-politicians-o, accessed July 19, 2016; Amy Sullivan, "Does Biden Have a Catholic Problem?" *Time*, September 13, 2008, http://content.time.com/time/politics/article/0,8599,1840965,00.html, accessed July 19, 2016.

the feelings and perceptions behind the scenes of this religious tradition's history in the United States and consider the experiences that defined—and continue to define—a generation even as the markers of that experience have faded.

For evidence of such experience, I turn to writers who have sought to describe this time and its effects. When writers reflect on pre–Vatican II Catholicism, they portray an integrated religious experience marked by authority in the multiple contexts of their lives. Perhaps exaggerated by the contrast to what they perceive in today's church, they show how life before this momentous council shaped them in ways that would be hard to relinquish, regardless of future belief or practice. This book examines the Catholic world depicted in these narratives and the distinct, but linked, settings that characterized it.

Cultural Catholicism—that is, a formative experience of growing up in the Roman Catholic tradition among a generation of Americans in the mid-twentieth century—is the subject of this study. While my own children may learn and even embrace the faith of their grandparents, the Catholicism they will inherit in this early part of the twenty-first century will be transmitted under notably different circumstances and therefore take remarkably different shape. Taking into account the recent scholarly and journalistic work on American Catholic life, my study addresses another set of questions pertaining to Catholic identity. Focusing on one particular generation, usually dubbed the Vatican II Catholics, I will explore their memories, representations, and depictions of their early years before that famed ecumenical council yielded enormous change. My book seeks to recapture a thickness of religious experience, one that linked the institutional church (parish and classroom), the home, and the neighborhood and that profoundly left its mark upon those who lived it. Drawing upon narrative literature on the subject, this book does not aim to classify any person as a "cultural Catholic";

instead, it recognizes a particular experience of this faith, one that went far beyond creeds and rituals. The phrase "cultural Catholicism," moreover, need not imply any particular level of affiliation and does not intend to convey any distance from the faith, like "lapsed Catholic" or "cafeteria Catholic" might. What matters is not what they believe or how they practice now, but rather what they learned and how they experienced their religion then. The depictions of these formative childhoods range from glowing nostalgia to deep-seated resentment. Still, writers curiously evidence the same shared types of powerfully formative experience.

Why "cultural Catholicism"? What is it about my parents' initiation into this faith that merits the term "cultural" any more than my daughter's childhood experiences do? As I will argue, the depictions of mid-twentieth-century Catholic upbringing reveal an all-encompassing, world-determining experience. Indeed, this was more than just participation in a church or a faith. It was a culture that defined one's life. As for my daughter's generation, no matter how much effort my husband and I might commit to her Catholic development and regardless of any cultural Catholic vestiges we might have picked up and passed along from the previous generation, her religious identity will ultimately be much more a product of deliberate formation than cultural surroundings. That is not to say, of course, that the parents of Vatican II Catholics did not work hard to practice the faith and instill it in their children; rather, there seemed to be no other choice. Today, we need only consult the latest Pew survey to discover that presumably my daughter will have nothing if not choice. What does it mean now in this time of choice to remember an ostensibly ubiquitous religion that prescribed one a personal identity without any alternative? This book offers an account of what it meant to be Catholic under those circumstances and how that cultural encounter might resonate for many American Catholics.

*Ingrained*
*Habits*

# Introduction

The sixth-grade teacher at my Catholic school was one of the most feared adults in the building. She was strict, calculated, and a committed educator. She was, of course, a nun. No one dared challenge Sr. Daria. Her modified habit, stern expression, and verbal precision earned her complete authority and deference. When she called me aside one day at recess, my mind raced to recall the offense I must have committed. It turned out that my great-uncle, Father William Purcell (known to my family as "Fr. Bill"), had stopped by the school while visiting my other great-uncle, his brother Monsignor Paul Purcell (known to my family as "Fr. Paul"), the current pastor of the parish. (My paternal grandmother had four brothers; three became diocesan priests.) I dutifully greeted Fr. Bill, whom I visited occasionally with my father. He always had a piece of candy or a present for his great-nieces and -nephews. This time he pulled out his wallet to give me a few dollars. Slightly embarrassed by the whole exchange and the attention it was receiving from the students and faculty on the playground, particularly Sr. Daria, I tried to be polite by refusing the gift. It was just nice to see him, I maturely asserted, sure that this behavior would win the approval of my teacher. He persisted. I caved and accepted the cash, hugged him good-bye and returned to my school day.

When we arrived back in the classroom, Sr. Daria called me

aside and, this time, did scold me. How dare I embarrass Father Purcell like that? As it turns out, the only polite thing would have been to accept the priest's gift graciously and thank him. A priest should be shown respect and gratitude for his generosity, not have to endure rude behavior in public. Mortified, I was stuck enduring a typical Sr. Daria admonishment after all; only this time it was the unexpected result of an interaction with my own uncle, who just happened to be one of my priest-uncles.

At eleven years old, this was the world I knew. It was a Catholic world in which children had constant interaction with vowed men and women. In 1988, the parish school could still boast some women religious at the helm. They accepted as their educational responsibilities not only providing religious and academic instruction but also imparting lessons about decorum in *all* contexts. Discipline was tightly woven into religious faith and ritual practice. Belief was learned through institutional structures where form seemed nearly as important as content. The power of the priest loomed large, and gender dynamics mattered. It was hard to imagine that anything existed outside this Catholic world.

Even if most of my classmates do not have tales of ordained uncles, they certainly have anecdotes about facing Sr. Daria's wrath. Whether instigated by an incomplete homework assignment or by unwelcome conduct in the cafeteria, her reprimands were experienced by nearly every student in my grade at some point before graduating from St. Paul's grade school. To be sure, my children will have schoolyard experiences bonding them with their classmates and with each other, but they will be much different than mine. Their stories will not involve nuns and priest-uncles. Indeed, when I think of my siblings and me as a type of bridge generation in our family, the specifics of my story become even more significant. I am certain my father has dozens of stories involving public encounters with the priest-uncles. My children will have none. The last of these priest-uncles has died, so the interactions they did have with him will likely be forgotten. The current numbers of ordained clergymen simply play against any likelihood that such a family legacy could continue. My husband and I have moved away from our childhood homes to the suburbs of Philadelphia, where our local parochial school has been one of many within the financially struggling archdiocese to close in the last few years. I am not sure when, or even if, my children will get the chance to know a nun in a substantive way. This does not make my baptized children any less Catholic, but it does make their introduction to and experience of the religion markedly different from those of preceding generations. Their initial encounter with this tradition will not be the all-encompassing one that characterized Catholic childhoods in earlier decades.

It was not until I was pursuing my Ph.D. in religious studies at a public university, far removed from my insular Catholic adolescence, that I realized the importance of my sixth-grade encounter. During my youth it seemed that every relationship I had was suffused with Catholicism, connecting me not only to networks of family but also to a broader community. As a graduate student, I began to see how many religious traditions did this and how American Catholicism functioned within a specific national history. As I developed this comparative and historical understanding, I also looked for specific archives to base my research. I stumbled upon a set of literary texts that described religious life in a way that felt familiar. What I found weren't tales of my childhood, though, but of childhoods before mine: novels and memoirs addressing Catholic existence in mid-twentieth-century America, a time before my own youth. Their circumstances included a pre–Vatican II church and a Catholic population making its way from the margins of American society. Even though this literature described conditions that were not mine, it communicated countless stories of characters, devotions, and expectations that painted curiously similar pictures of Catholic life and included situations to which I could relate. I began to understand my childhood encounter with Catholicism as a vestige of this earlier period, an inherited version of a tradition. Mine was not just a religious birthright but a cultural inheritance, marked by institution, story, structure, discipline, and ritual. It had its roots in a church that was in the midst of decades-long change. I felt linked to this writing cohort through an experience of Catholicism that extended far beyond creed and that was changing with every passing decade.

This book explores the concept of cultural Catholicism—an experience rooted in a Catholic upbringing characterized by an all-encompassing encounter with religion. Catholics who once inhabited such a world may feel far from the actual time and place of it, but its lessons and presumptions remain firmly part of their makeup. They recall their tradition's bearing on nearly every aspect of their lives, from recess encounters to parental relationships to professional aspirations. Regardless of their current religious affiliation and practice today, participants in a past cultural Catholicism claim a shared religious history that formed them.

Scholars in recent decades have used the terms "cultural Catholic" and "communal Catholic" as labels for individuals who grew up with Catholicism and were deeply affected by it but no longer have a definitive connection to the church or even reject the church altogether. Such attention contributes significantly to our awareness of and larger conversations about the complicated relationship between Catholic life and American culture over the last few centuries. Thomas Ferraro, for example, writes in his essay "Not-Just-Cultural Catholics," "As a catchphrase, 'cultural Catholicism' suggests the development and deployment of Catholic ways of knowing and habits of being outside the official precincts and sanction, if not purview, of the Church." He explains that as Catholics move further away from their religious origins into more secular environments, they gain new perspective but retain old habits: "The national *habitus* affords critical distance on the Church and its members, yet even the criticism that ensues may exhibit Catholic modalities, tutored in the catechism and confessional, of course, but also in the pews, playgrounds, kitchens, bedrooms, and hospitals, where the lay practicum—including much of its mysticism—really happens."[1] No matter how far they might stray from their Catholicism, he suggests, it follows them and manifests itself in unexpected ways.

Perhaps the best-known author on the subject is sociologist and priest Andrew Greeley, who wrote extensively about a trend among some Americans who maintain a Catholic identity despite growing distance from the church.[2] Greeley writes that in the mid-twentieth century, "Catholicism had, so to speak, two faces—the one of Sacrament and celebration and community, the other of rules and enforcement."[3] He contends that the latter has driven people away but that despite such estrangement from the church, these people maintain a Catholic identity. Greeley resolves to understand why so many people who disagree with the church stay Catholic and to distinguish the changes the church needs to make to keep its members for the long run. Ultimately, he finds one answer to both questions: the beauty of the tradition's stories, images, and rituals. He credits a "sacramental imagination"—by which people recognize God's presence in everyday life—with keeping people connected to their religious tradition. They have gotten used to experiencing the divine in daily activities and they like it. Greeley writes, "Religion

---

1. Thomas J. Ferraro, "Not-Just-Cultural Catholics," *Catholic Lives, Contemporary America* (Durham, N.C.: Duke University Press, 1997), 9.

2. See for example, Andrew M. Greeley, *The Catholic Imagination* (Berkeley: University of California Press, 2000); Greeley, *The Communal Catholic: A Personal Manifesto* (New York: Seabury, 1976).

3. Andrew M. Greeley, *The Catholic Revolution: New Wine, Old Wineskins, and the Second Vatican Council* (Berkeley: University of California Press, 2004), 29.

is experience, image and story before it is anything else and after it is everything else. Catholics like their heritage because it has great stories."[4] The problem, he argues, is that the focus has moved away from the beauty and charm of Catholicism's stories, and, for the church to survive, it needs to put them back at the center of Catholic life.

Such scholarly attention to grown Catholics' relationship with the church and their religious heritage raises crucial questions for my own work. It detects something particular about this religious tradition that seems to remain with people even when they move well beyond the actual context of belief or practice. Indeed, many of the authors under study here might self-identify in that category; however, the focus in this work is not so much their current position on the church, level of adherence, or likelihood for return. Instead, it looks to the commonly shared past among those across the spectrum of current faith and praxis, ranging from declared atheists to practicing priests. Even with widely divergent attitudes toward their current church, the authors under study here depict a common history within it. Rather than consider the concept of "cultural Catholics" who have moved away from the institution, my research considers the "cultural Catholicism" of the past. The evidence in these texts indicates not two separate faces of Catholicism, but one culture of religion in which celebration and community seemed inextricably linked with the rules and enforcement, and all aspects blended into regular routines.

Another recent area of scholarship that clears a path for my work has been the careful attention to the Catholic laity's encounter with institutional and demographic change over the course of the twentieth century. For example, in *The Faithful: A History of Catholics in America*, James O'Toole identifies six distinct historical periods for the church and focuses on a particular person's expe-

4. Ibid., 105.

rience of each period to illuminate its impact. In *Prayers of the Faithful: The Shifting Spiritual Life of American Catholics*, James P. McCartin looks closely at transforming prayer life across the 1900s as a way of studying large-scale changes that occurred over the century. Colleen McDannell traces her own mother's history to examine the effects of the Second Vatican Council in *The Spirit of Vatican II: A History of Catholic Reform in America*. These texts both emphasize the dramatic shifts the American church experienced throughout the twentieth century and highlight the role of and effect upon people in the pews. They offer broad histories of the church's century through particular encounters with its major transitions. By outlining the overarching narratives on the Catholic Church and the fundamental changes that occurred for its members throughout the twentieth century, such research invites investigation into particular moments along the way. In this study, I focus the lens closely on a generation of Catholics to grasp what everyday life was like in certain places at a certain time. By observing intimate encounters with religion, I aim to identify those features perceived to be characteristic aspects of growing up Catholic during the middle decades of the last century among those who write about it. In his conclusion to *The Faithful*, James O'Toole writes:

Had some miracle of time travel permitted our six American Catholics to sit together and talk, they would have found that they had much in common. They would have recognized the same basic elements in the practice of their religion, including the Mass, the sacraments, and the way they prayed. At the same time, they would have noticed differences in their experiences, the products of their own particular times and circumstances. Still, they would have known that together they embodied the American Catholic laity. As these experiences continue to change, understanding them in the past helps us understand the future.[5]

5. James M. O'Toole, *The Faithful: A History of Catholics in America* (Cambridge, Mass.: Belknap Press of Harvard University Press, 2010), 308.

As the American Catholic laity proceeds into the twenty-first century within an ever-changing church, they might learn where they are and what they face ahead by looking closely at their past. This book looks at that past.

To access that past, or at least memories of its defining features, I turn back to this body of written work, which has received minimal scholarly attention, even as many of its authors have achieved national and international fame. Writers have narrated their versions of a pre–Vatican II American Catholic world. Through such stories, readers gain admission to the spaces where religion was conveyed through routines of daily life. Authors ultimately portray the world that produced a cultural Catholicism—something my generation might experience through inadvertent remnants passed along and my children's generation would only know as a result of intentional choices. Through analyzing these stories, this book begins to outline the dimensions of that cultural Catholicism. I have limited my sources to selections of prose, but I do similarly treat works designated as fiction and nonfiction. While I have no intention of erasing the difference between novels and memoir, the writers' portrayals of Catholic environments, real or imagined, are what matter for this study. Further, I focus on published accounts of these settings rather than archival documents, which produce a body of literature with a few noteworthy aspects. First, these stories have been specifically composed for a public audience, even if they do share personal, intimate details. This suggests that authors construct the contents with intended significance for presumed readers, creating a deliberate picture of Catholic life. Second, this collection of sources largely depends on the memory of its authors. While that might compromise the accuracy of certain accounts, what matters more for the purpose of this investigation is how the authors perceive the experience and thereby emphasize the most influential parts of that religious world.

In his scholarly perspective on this subject, Robert Orsi adds another element to the cause and effect of such public remembering. In *Between Heaven and Earth*, he writes about the generation of Catholics who grew up in the mid-twentieth century: "The members of no other religious community in the United States return so compulsively to their past."[6] He contends that this was actually a consequence of trying to move beyond that past. He claims, "The culture that tried to build so high a barrier against the past wound up creating an obsessive culture of memory. . . . Memory became not the practice of engaging the past but another medium for fending it off and keeping it distant. Catholic 'remembering' since the 1960s has assumed the task of denying the past for some, and for others of celebrating and canonizing the past, and as a result the lived complexity of the past, especially of the devotional past, was lost." This discovery came through his own research on devotion to St. Jude, which he says "fell right into the rupture that Catholics were so assiduously enforcing between present and past."[7] Once again, such recognition of and attention to this generation of Catholics and their relationships to this religion deeply enrich the scholarly discussion of American Catholicism over the last several decades. Moreover, the impetus for and consequence of remembering certainly affect the narratives shared and the reception by readers, which is an important reminder as I engage these texts. Still, my focus remains not on the motivating factors for this type of literature or even the effect upon the authors of writing it. Instead, I look closely at a wide range of writing, not only those solely focused on the writers' religious pasts, to draw out the shared details that create a picture of a Catholic upbringing during the middle decades of the twentieth century. Inevitably, some written sources do align with Orsi's characterization of adults fixated on either denying or

---

6. Robert A. Orsi, *Between Heaven and Earth: The Religious Worlds People Make and the Scholars Who Study Them* (Princeton: Princeton University Press, 2005), 155.

7. Ibid., 156.

celebrating their Catholic pasts, but most are telling broader stories that necessarily feature this consuming aspect of their early lives. In either remembering their personal histories or drawing characters in their fiction, the deeply entrenched Catholicism of their youth emerges in ways that shine light on the details of that experience. As I continue to witness change in my own Catholic experience and observe my children's early encounters with the church, I intend to mine these writings as a means of accessing the same for my parents' generation decades ago.

While perusing these texts, readers need to be wary of the sometimes seductive nature of their stories. The good-old, and even not-so-good-old, days can easily entice a reader into a kind of wistfulness for the past when things were clear-cut: right and wrong, us and them. By remembering those circumstances through a reminiscent filter, readers might easily overlook the potentially detrimental effects of such a strict Catholic environment. It remains crucial not to forget that these narratives may obscure harsher realities among those who suffered within these circumstances, even as the same stories allow others to connect fondly with a familiar history.

Most of the authors under study were born between 1940 and 1965 and self-identify as having been raised Catholic. This precludes anyone with origins in a different faith tradition, including converts to Catholicism. Authors like Mary Gordon, Alice McDermott, and Patricia Hampl were part of this generation of "Vatican II Catholics," as they have been labeled by some, but no longer occupy the circumstances of their childhood religious settings. No one could. Nevertheless, from their narrative positions, these authors offer a window onto the details that shaped that experience. This generational cohort has received much attention recently as a result of the terrible revelations of sexual abuse by Catholic clergy during this period. These tragic circumstances sadly affect many cohorts of Catholics, but this generation seems to have been particularly victimized. This project in no way intends to minimize this reality, and I recognize that some conditions of Catholic life highlighted in my sources (the unquestioned primacy of priests, for example) undoubtedly contributed to the environments that allowed this to happen. Still, because this dimension of American Catholic history does not contribute to the cultural Catholicism under study, stories of these horrific encounters will not be directly considered. The victims' suffering and the church's continued efforts to deal with this painful reality remind us that history can never be neatly simplified. So this project turns its attention to one aspect of the many that made up this complicated time in the American Catholic story.

This study does not address all Catholic experience across the United States during the mid-twentieth century. In part as a consequence of its sources and their emphases, it focuses heavily on urban life in the Northeast and Midwest. Although gender and class will appear regularly in the study to follow as topics within this literature, race does not. In particular, the specific story of African American Catholics is not explored. As many African Americans moved from Southern states into Northern cities during the twentieth century, they were excluded from the ethnically constructed communities that emerged from the immigrant Catholic church. While black Catholics have written important works that detail childhood experiences, African Americans have not produced the same volume of narratives as those with European heritage about early life in the church during this time period. Those African American stories about growing up Catholic in the mid-twentieth century that have been published to date offer compelling reflections and offer vital perspectives on such a complicated history, calling for further scholarly attention.[8] African American silence

8. This study does consider Donna Brazile, *Cooking with Grease: Stirring the Pots in American Politics* (New York: Simon and Schuster, 2004); see also Kareem Abdul Jabbar and Peter Knobler, *Giant Steps: The Autobiography of Kareem Abduul Jabbar* (New York: Ban-

in this study, though, speaks loudly to the broader issue of race in American Catholic history. Worshiping in the universal church and learning its faith, young black Catholics experienced a much different introduction to Catholicism than their white peers. Racially segregated seating within churches or altogether segregated churches during mid-century made it difficult to feel like a real part of this religious community. Even in recent years, black Catholics have felt the need to argue for the authenticity of their race and their religion, a minority within a minority.[9] These circumstances contribute to a distancing of African Americans from the cultural Catholicism that emerges in much literature about that time and that is under study here. Moreover, white authors who narrate that mid-century world rarely deal with the issue of race. It is possible that the segregated nature of Catholic life allowed them a certain naiveté about their larger context during childhood; or maybe they have chosen to overlook that dimension of the experience. It remains hard to tell. In either case, this study reflects that same silence on the topic, but acknowledges the absence of those voices and the wounds inflicted by such exclusion. African Americans claim a Catholicism for which they have had to fight, even among their fellow Catholics. This analysis considers the opposite experience whereby, among Catholics, one's religious affiliation felt like a foregone conclusion.

Recognizing the demographic scope of this work, my analysis focuses on a perceived authority and prescribed identity emphasized in accounts of Catholic youth in the mid-twentieth century.

tam, 1983); Jean K. Douglas, *Why I Left the Church, Why I Came Back, and Why I Just Might Leave Again: Memories of Growing Up African American and Catholic* (Astor, Fla.: Fortuity, 2006); Jacqueline Jordan Irvine and Michele Foster, eds., *Growing Up African American in Catholic Schools* (New York: Teachers College Press, 1996); Charles B. Rangel with Leon Wynter, *And I Haven't Had a Bad Day Since: From the Streets of Harlem to the Halls of Congress* (New York: Thomas Dunne, 2007); Jo Anne Tardy, *A Light Will Rise in the Darkness: Growing Up Black and Catholic in New Orleans* (Skokie, Ill.: ACTA, 2006).

9. See C. Vanessa White, "Authentically Black and Truly Catholic," September 5, 2010, http://www.cnn.com/2010/OPINION/09/05/white.catholic.black.html, accessed July 7, 2016.

It locates three specific contexts for such interaction: the institutional church in the form of the parish and school; the home; and the neighborhood. It then explores how each setting contained its own lessons for what it meant to be Catholic during this period. As the book works its way through these three fundamental sites, with a chapter devoted to each, readers observe the ways this religious tradition was felt to permeate all aspects of daily life.

Chapter 1 offers a historical approach to the circumstances of the mid-twentieth century among American Catholics. Using the work of historians, the chapter introduces such issues as the role of the parochial school, the place of religious devotions, the socioeconomic status of American Catholics, the significance of the Second Vatican Council, and the ethnic dimension of religious practice. These conditions comprised the backdrop for Catholic life. Those who lived among such conditions would have hardly noticed them, but most of existence would have been determined by them.

The book then moves into the narratives themselves to examine specific contexts where Catholicism was learned and internalized through personal encounter. Chapter 2 addresses the institutional church in the form of the parish and parochial school as depicted in this literature. In the classrooms and the pews, boys and girls absorbed lessons involving not only sacrament and sin, but structure and etiquette. High expectations were established to ensure that discipline became a key factor in religious practice as well as in routine interactions. Faith passed on through ritual demanded proper posture, technique, and attitude. For many children, these aspects of religious observance blended naturally with the beliefs behind them.

Chapter 3 moves into the realm of the home. In these intimate spaces, where children would first be introduced to the tradition, they observed a Catholicism lived outside the institution. Devotions, objects, and habits added another dimension to their Catholic identities. Gendered norms, sexual mores, and filial expectations expanded religious reality to something deeply personal that had lasting impacts on their own senses of self, their relationships, and their religious identities.

Chapter 4 explores the streets of the neighborhood. These public areas have been widely portrayed as religiously and ethnically homogeneous communities that inevitably issued an identity to their youngest inhabitants. One's geography seemed, to them, to determine their religious affiliation and the nature of its practice. Moreover, ethnic and religious identity could become inextricably linked so that to profess a connection to the first meant automatic membership in the second. With numerous European immigrant groups settling in American cities and building their churches, the literature does tend to emphasize the experience of Irish and Italian Catholics. Other ethnic groups will be considered, but, mostly as a consequence of the sources, the chapter highlights those influential communities.

The Roman Catholic Church is an ever-changing institution. Currently, Catholics are living within a church led by Pope Francis, whose message and priorities seem to diverge from some of his predecessors'. Clearly, we need not look far to witness the ongoing transformations of this universal church and its American context. This book invites readers to consider one dimension of what it has meant to be Catholic in the United States. During a time when religion seemed predictable and unquestionable, mid-twentieth-century Catholicism provided the lens for understanding the world and clear guidelines for acting within it. Catholics still embrace the tradition's lens and its guidelines, but the emphases and surrounding contexts have dramatically shifted. The generation that followed experienced some elements of a pre–Vatican II Catholic world, but today's Catholic children experience this religious tradition within a vastly different structure. This book explores the features of a cultural Catholicism that defined a particular initiation into the faith and a sense of identity for those who lived it.

# CHAPTER 1

## How Come You're Not
## Named after a Saint?

࿇

*Growing Up Catholic in*
*Mid-Twentieth-Century*
*America*

Kids can be cruel on elementary school playgrounds. In 1950s Queens, New York, Claudia DeMonte felt the pain of regular teasing by her classmates. The focus of her peers' jabs, though, might surprise some. Her fellow students at Our Lady of Mt. Carmel would shout, "How come you're not named after a saint? Claudia's not a saint's name. It's against church law not to be named after a saint."[1] Such jeering was apparently part of being Catholic for someone like her, born in 1947. Claudia survived this pesky harassment and went on to become a successful artist. For her and many like her, who grew up Catholic in the mid-twentieth-century United States, the world was a place where children heckled each

1. Claudia DeMonte, "The Whole World Was Italian," in *Growing Up Italian: How Being Brought Up as an Italian-American Helped Shape the Characters, Lives and Fortunes of Twenty-Four Celebrated Americans*, ed. Linda Brandi Cateura (New York: William and Morrow, 1987), 54.

other about saints on the playground and parochial schools ruled the day. It was a time when Catholics were living in (or leaving) ethnic enclaves and learning how to engage with their American surroundings. This chapter offers an introduction to the historical context for the time period considered in this book. Invoking different voices and examples, I will sketch a broad outline of the milieu in which Catholic life took shape for so many families. This outline introduces the three main contexts: (1) the institutional church, consisting of the parish and parochial school, where priests and nuns exuded authority; (2) the family home, where parents and grandparents modeled prayer and expectations; and (3) the ethnic neighborhood, where religious identity came with the territory. These constitute the key sites in literary depictions of a formative Catholicism.

The Catholic Church has long held a presence in what has become the United States, but it was in the mid-nineteenth century that its population witnessed notable growth. Circumstances in Europe during these decades, combined with opportunity here, yielded a major boom of European Catholic immigrants to the United States.[2] They arrived to face some challenging conditions, and they brought with them some of their own. As the religious minority in a Protestant nation, Catholics faced strong resistance to their presence in this new place, and they had little infrastructure on which to lean. So, they had to build it themselves. Historian Jay Dolan succinctly states, "The key institution in this organizational process was the parish."[3] Religiously and socially, the parish be-

2. For more on this historical development, see Jay P. Dolan, *The Immigrant Church: New York's Irish and German Catholics, 1815–1865* (Notre Dame, Ind.: University of Notre Dame Press, 1992); James T. Fisher, *Communion of Immigrants: A History of Catholics in America* (Oxford: Oxford University Press, 2002); Jeffrey M. Burns, Ellen Skerrett, and Joseph M. White, eds., *Keeping Faith: European and Asian Catholic Immigrants*, American Catholic Identities: A Documentary History (Maryknoll, N.Y.: Orbis, 2000).

3. Jay P. Dolan, *The American Catholic Experience: A History from Colonial Times to the Present* (Garden City, N.Y.: Doubleday, 1985), 159.

came the center of their communities. Among these new American Catholics, however, the diversity of their origins became problematic. Wanting to worship and converse in their own languages as well as preserve customs from their countries, Catholics from different places in Europe began to construct their own respective parishes. Since families contributed to the organization and construction of these churches and found a kind of belonging and safety within their communities, the growth of the Catholic Church ultimately created a pattern for ethnic enclaves. This would, for the most part, remain the paradigm until the mid-twentieth century, when American demographics began to shift and upward mobility became a viable option for Roman Catholics.

From the middle of the nineteenth century through the middle of the twentieth century, the establishment of an immigrant church in a mostly Protestant nation yielded another important institution for American Catholics: the parochial school. The history of the parochial school system in the United States involved complicated religious and political debates as it developed. Such larger organizational concerns, though, would have had little impact on the children whose lives were being incomparably shaped by Catholic schooling.

Volumes of historical research document and analyze the complex developments of parishes and schools in American Catholic history. For the purposes of this work, I only mention this background because it constitutes the historical setting for literary depictions of the middle decades of the twentieth century. Ultimately, that time period would witness the slow shift away from this fairly insulated Catholic structure to the more assimilated one we recognize now. Such change happens slowly, though. Scholar Robert Orsi suggests that it happened across two gradual transformations: one concerned the demographic shift in which second-, third-, and fourth-generation American Catholics were moving from the city to the suburbs. The second transformation involved the religious shift in which Catholics were grappling with the liturgical reforms prompted by Vatican II.[4] The neighborhoods would begin to look and feel different, and so would the church. My children will experience a vastly different Catholic upbringing from that of my parents. Still, while a historical perspective might produce a story of large-scale change throughout these years, a literary perspective on those decades accessed through written depictions of the time shares a more intimate setting of daily life.

Simply put, for most Catholics in the 1940s, '50s, and '60s, life revolved around the church and its stories. Devotions, religious images, and feast and fast days blended into the settings and rhythms of regular life. Even as certain practices may have risen and fallen in popularity, they had a way of ingraining undeniable habits.[5] These events, interpretations, and actions became part of the expected routine. Doris Kearns Goodwin (b. 1943) remembers lying awake on Christmas Eve, "listening as the thunder of church bells at midnight announced the coming of the Savior" and dreaming of when she might be old enough to join her sisters for Midnight Mass. Later in the liturgical calendar, receiving ashes at the start of Lent seemed to coincide with Kearns's nightly prayer: "Now I lay me down to sleep, I pray the Lord my soul to keep. If I should die before I wake, I pray the Lord my soul to take."[6] With such seamless integration into life, the church's ritual and symbolism ostensibly enveloped Catholics' existence.

4. Orsi, *Between Heaven and Earth*, 8.

5. For an in-depth consideration of different forms and developments, see James M. O'Toole, ed., *Habits of Devotion: Catholic Religious Practice in Twentieth-Century America*, Cushwa Center Studies of Catholicism in Twentieth-Century America (Ithaca, N.Y.: Cornell University Press, 2004).

6. Doris Kearns Goodwin, "The Brooklyn Dodgers and the Catholic Church," in *I Like Being Catholic: Treasured Traditions, Ritual, and Stories*, ed. Michael Leach and Therese J. Borchard (New York: Doubleday, 2000), 68.

## The Institutional Church

In the written stories of everyday life, a few spaces and places emerge consistently. Given the church's immigrant boom and the centrality of the parish in Catholics' efforts to establish their place and future, the local church inevitably features prominently in literary representations. Historian Charles Morris explains: "In its glory days, especially in the 1940s and 1950s, the Catholic Church constructed a virtual state-within-a-state so Catholics could live almost their entire lives within a thick cocoon of Catholic institutions."[7] The parish rested at the heart of this cultural bubble and issued a calendar to follow, social activities in which to participate, and religious practice to structure one's way of life. For children born into this system, there seemed to exist little beyond it. Even if there were anything else, who needed it? Life felt safe, controlled, and predictable. Author Anna Quindlen (b. 1953) recalls the totalizing nature of it in the moments that marked life: "I was educated by nuns, given absolution by priests. My parents were married in a Catholic church, my grandparents and mother buried from one. Saturday afternoons kneeling on Leatherette pads in the dim light of the confessional, listening for the sound of the priest sliding back the grille on his side. Sunday mornings kneeling with my face in my hands, the Communion wafer stuck to the roof of my dry mouth. These are my history."[8] Whether in the major life events or the week-to-week habits, the church existed at the center of things. Artist Claudia DeMonte reflects on a particular celebration her family enjoyed, the special devotion to her father's patron saint: "Each year on his name day, St. Joseph's feast day on March 19, we used to send him special greeting cards and eat zeppole di San Gi-

7. Charles R. Morris, *American Catholic: The Saints and Sinners Who Built America's Most Powerful Church* (New York: Times Books, 1997), vii.

8. Anna Quindlen, *Living Out Loud* (New York: Ballantine, 1994), 158.

useppe all day."[9] For author John Grogan's family, March's importance was similarly recognized: "I came along in 1957. John Joseph. Mom and Dad were hoping I would be a Saint Patrick's Day baby. When I missed that date, they rooted for Saint Joseph's Day, which would have been fitting, given all our middle names (Josephine, Joseph and Joseph). Late again."[10] Saints' days were one of the central means of marking time. There were traditions and practices that came along with each of them, so that life seemed to revolve around the church and its narratives.

In the decades following World War I, devotional practice was a prominent factor in Catholicism. This took various forms, but most popular were devotions to the Virgin Mary in the rosary, in novenas, and in special feast days celebrating her apparitions. Anne Rice (b. 1941) recalls how such ritual punctuated her weekdays as a child. She writes, "One key church service dominates all others except for the Mass. Every Tuesday night . . . there was a novena service to Our Mother of Perpetual Help." She notes that most churches held services weekly, allowing the participants to figure out how and when to attend nine in a row, the requirement for a novena. She recalls that at her parish, "usually there were some hundred or so crowding the dark wooden pews."[11] Adoration of the Eucharist, frequent Communion, and (therefore) frequent confession also experienced a resurgence during these decades. Starting in the early part of the twentieth century and continuing through those middle decades, the pastoral technique of "retreats" offered another popular option. These retreats featured a weekend of prayer and devotional rituals for lay men and lay women under the leadership of ordained priests or nuns.[12] Such a diverse collection of practices

9. DeMonte, "Whole World Was Italian," 54.

10. John Grogan, *The Longest Trip Home: A Memoir* (New York: Harper, 2008), 9.

11. Anne Rice, *Called Out of Darkness: A Spiritual Confession* (New York: Anchor, 2008), 20–21.

12. For more on devotional Catholicism during this time period, see the following

could easily occupy any Catholic and ensured that the local parish and the vowed members of the church remained prominent features of one's life.

For children, another branch of the institutional church became the center of religious experience: the parochial school. This educational system, with each school run by its local Catholic parish, took precedence among American Catholics during the 1940s, '50s, and '60s. Historian Colleen McDannell writes, "Between 1945 and 1962 Catholic school enrollment increased by 129 percent while the general public school population rose by only 69 percent."[13] This proved to be another site of transition over the decades. Catholic school population would peak in the mid-1960s and decrease significantly over the next half century.[14] Today newspaper headlines about parochial school closures evidence another fundamental contrast between Catholic life then and now. Varied circumstances have contributed to this shift, not least of which has been the enormous decline of Catholic sisters who commonly staffed these schools.

For many young Catholic parents today witnessing rising tuition rates and diminishing numbers of Catholic schools, it might be difficult to fathom the seemingly universal decision to send children to parochial school in the mid-twentieth century. Chapter 2 will address the place of parish schools in remembered depictions of Catholic life. Ranging in tone from nostalgic fondness to embittered resentment, the stories indicate an essential place for this

books by James P. Dolan: *American Catholic Experience*, 384–88; *American Catholic Parish: A History from 1850 to the Present* (New York: Paulist Press, 1987), 2:345–46; *In Search of an American Catholicism: A History of Religion and Culture in Tension* (Oxford and New York: Oxford University Press, 2002), 168–73; as well as O'Toole, *Faithful*, 145–265.

13. Colleen McDannell, *The Spirit of Vatican II: A History of Catholic Reform in America* (New York: Basic Books, 2011), 47.

14. Thomas Hunt, "Historical Overview of Catholic Schools in the United States," in *Catholic Schools in the United States: An Encyclopedia*, ed. Thomas Hunt, Ellis A. Joseph, and Ronald J. Nuzzi (Westport, Conn.: Greenwood, 2004), 4.

experience in young people's lives at the time. Still, it might help readers who did not live through that period to appreciate the motivating factors that would have encouraged parents to send their children to parochial school and to get a closer look at the religious and social context for doing so.

If we take seriously the leading experts on Catholic schools at the time, there would have been good reason for enrolling children in Catholic schools. First, their goal of seamlessly combining academics with faith development relieved parents of some of this responsibility. In 1961, Fr. Leo Ward of the University of Notre Dame claimed that the Catholic school's ideal was to integrate completely the work of educating children with the task of forming Christians. "Faith and fractions are almost as if out of the same book," he wrote.[15] As Catholic parents were forging into the American way of life through their advances in the work force and social classes, they probably recognized in their children a great potential for bringing Catholicism into many aspects of American culture. There was a growing feeling that Catholics could achieve success in the United States without abandoning their religious tradition and community.[16] Therefore, if these students could appropriately learn that their faith was innately connected to all other parts of life, they might successfully influence their national culture with a desirable dose of Catholicism—a prominent goal among Catholics of the mid-century.

Along these lines, the schools could also bolster the children's growing awareness of specific Catholic religious rituals and practices. In her reflections on the duties of the parochial school principal during this time, Sister M. Jerome Corcoran expressed how her contemporaries assumed this responsibility: "Religious practice . . . is a subtle influence which most directly concerns the parochial

15. Leo R. Ward, "Principles for Principals," introduction to *The Catholic Elementary School Principal*, by Sister M. Jerome Corcoran (Milwaukee: Bruce, 1961), 10.
16. See Dolan, *In Search of an American Catholicism*, 152.

school. Parochial school teachers meet such instances of remissness as the following: Kathy is consistently absent from Sunday Mass, Jimmy brings meat in his lunch on Friday, Eddie is missing when the Scouts have their Communion Sunday."[17] In 1961, the faculty and administrators assumed the responsibility for *subtly* influencing their students' religious adherence even when it did not directly affect the school day. In fact, their adherence could not be limited even to the church, but was evidenced by their lunchbox or their extracurricular activities. Certainly, this kind of attention from educators ensured pupils learned all aspects of their religion. It would also create an atmosphere in which children's religious life extended well beyond school walls and was always under close inspection.

One more appealing aspect of the parochial school was the moral guidance it imparted to the youth. Father Ward explains that within every child is the power of freedom, but that most children do not know what do with such power. Here is where the parochial school offers an advantage: "With the aid of doctrines and liturgy and sacraments, the child can be guided along lines that will enable him to begin to develop the power." There were distinct steps for developing one's ability to deal with freedom. Among them was what Ward labeled "built-in habits." He explains: "The child is, above all, learning to be generous and self-sacrificial. . . . He is learning to understand both how to *be good* and that *being good* and *doing good* is *itself* a *good thing*."[18] Generosity and self-sacrifice were teachable habits in the Catholic school, according to Fr. Ward, and they demanded attention and effort. With any success, these teachers inculcated an aptitude and appreciation for "being good"—however that might have been interpreted. The promised help with regard to moral education of their children likely offered relief for parents working to be both good Catholics and respectable Americans.

17. Corcoran, *Catholic Elementary School Principal*, 294.
18. Ward, "Principles for Principals," 12.

Such influential work would demand qualified teachers. Sister Corcoran explains principals' priority for hiring and training teachers: "Even before we say what a good teacher should *do*, we must know what she *is* as a person."[19] Students learning to be good Catholics would need good Catholic examples to follow, and, for this reason, there was significant emphasis on the personal character of every teacher, most of whom were nuns during this period. Throughout the 1930s and 1940s, men and women from different religious orders staffed the growing parochial school system almost exclusively as teachers and principals.[20] In his analysis of these decades of American Catholic life, scholar Robert Orsi explains, "Whatever desires, intentions, or dreams drew these adults into the religious life in the first place, their most insistent responsibility and challenge in the twentieth century was to supervise the religious formation of children."[21] Clearly dedicated to their religious institution, they set high standards for their pupils. Starting in the 1950s and continuing to the present, nuns' presence in the classroom has declined, in tandem with their decline in vocations. Lay teachers have replaced them. Since the process took a few decades and only accelerated after Vatican II, the children attending schools during the 1950s and into the 1960s would have barely felt its impact. This atmosphere, characterized by education, observation, and example and created by nuns, determined the daily life of most Catholic children born during the 1940s, '50s, and '60s and, as their literature demonstrates, left an impression.[22]

19. Corcoran, *Catholic Elementary School Principal*, 182.

20. In 1936, out of a total of 58,903 teachers in Catholic elementary schools, 55,467 were religious (94 percent); see Harold A. Buetow, *Of Singular Benefit: The Story of Catholic Education in the United States* (New York: Macmillan, 1970), 226.

21. Orsi, *Between Heaven and Earth*, 82.

22. For more on Catholic schools, see James Youniss, John J. Convey, and Jeffrey A. McLellan, *The Catholic Character of Catholic Schools* (Notre Dame, Ind.: University of Notre Dame Press, 2000); James Youniss and John J. Convey, *Catholic Schools at the Crossroads: Survival and Transformation* (New York: Teachers College Press, 2000); Anthony S. Bryk,

## The Family Home

The parish and the school served as central axes for practice and formation, but naturally the home served as a foundational environment for a Catholic upbringing during the mid-twentieth century. After all, here was where religion and religious identity would have been first introduced and integrated into the ordinary routine. This would have included not only creed and ritual but also a perceived inherited identity and its ramifications for involvement in the American experience.

Novelist Alice McDermott (b. 1953) reflects on her own family's religious character: "My father carried a worn scapular. My mother put a holy card of Saint Jude in the back window whenever she was praying for good weather. One of my brothers was an altar boy, the other spoke about becoming a priest. We ate spaghetti with tomato sauce on Friday nights." Looking back on this reality, she observes, "We were Catholics as inevitably as we were ourselves: the McDermott family on Emily Avenue, and with about as much self-consciousness and, it seemed, volition."[23] Her depiction emphasizes the deep integration of Catholicism into even the banal particulars of life. It was what they did and who they were. At the time, there appeared little need to think about it and little choice for doing otherwise. It is this kind of recollection that typifies so many of the stories about Catholic childhoods of the time, when religion simply surrounded one always and everywhere. The dynamics at home as they are depicted in these stories provide another crucial access point into this time in American Catholic history.

Once again, the decades leading into the middle part of the

---

Valerie E. Lee, and Peter Blakeley Holland, *Catholic Schools and the Common Good* (Cambridge, Mass.: Harvard University Press, 1993); Buetow, *Of Singular Benefit*.

23. Alice McDermott, "Confessions of a Reluctant Catholic: Portrait of a Novelist," *Commonweal* 127, no. 3 (2000): 12.

century would establish certain factors for how Catholic identity would be perceived, embodied, and shared among family members in their homes. From the time the church made its way to this country, its members struggled with fitting into the larger society while maintaining the religion's institutional integrity. What has been deemed the "Americanist controversy" pitted Catholics against one another in the 1890s regarding the level to which Catholics and the church itself should have adapted to life in the United States.[24] Such internal debates yielded varying levels of Catholic accommodation to American circumstances. Conditions external to Catholic communities also had enormous impact at the turn and early decades of the twentieth century. Catholics' patriotic allegiance and their prominence among labor unions did allow them to participate in important political and social issues. Still, even as these developments were happening, the American Protective Association, an openly anti-Catholic group, was busy registering over one million members during the 1890s.[25] By the turn of the century, this organization had fallen apart, but then Catholics faced another threat in the Ku Klux Klan, who professed hatred for blacks, Catholics, Jews, and all foreigners and enjoyed a resurgence of membership during the 1920s.

Despite these organized anti-Catholic efforts, Catholics still made their way to the center of American politics by the end of the 1920s, and Catholic families were certainly paying attention. By winning the Democratic nomination during the presidential election year of 1928, Alfred Smith, a Catholic from New York, pushed Catholics into

24. For studies of the Americanist controversy among Catholics at the turn of the twentieth century and surrounding issues, see Thomas Timothy McAvoy, *The Americanist Heresy in Roman Catholicism, 1895–1900* (Notre Dame, Ind.: University of Notre Dame Press, 1963); John T. McGreevy, *Catholicism and American Freedom: A History* (New York: W. W. Norton, 2003), 91–165; Morris, *American Catholic*, 81–138.

25. See McGreevy, *Catholicism and American Freedom*, 124.

the national public eye.[26] It was becoming possible to be both entirely democratic and affiliated with the monarchical institution of the Catholic Church. Alfred Smith lost the presidential election, and historian John McGreevy reports that anti-Catholicism proved the decisive issue for voter behavior.[27] Despite this perceived setback for Catholics in the public sphere, they were indeed advancing into the American cultural and intellectual mainstreams. Though parents and children may not have fully understood its impact while it was happening, these movements affected daily life.

In the early days, Catholicism made immigrants a target for nativist mistreatment; however, it also provided them their community and their strength. Their faith seemed to reward them as they slowly ascended the ranks in society. While it set them apart, it simultaneously designated them as part of this committed group who believed and practiced and who could also contribute to society. These circumstances seeped into family homes. With the parish at the center of their developing infrastructures, parents extended the church into intimate spaces. This ensured that the faith would continue and that the surrounding communities would be influenced—positively, from their perspective—by the Catholics they were raising. The nomination and election of John F. Kennedy in 1960 would be a grand symbol for the culmination of this process in the minds of most American Catholics.

In day-to-day life, though, their political and socioeconomic standing was not the primary focus of the household. Instead prayers, practices, expectations, and visual reminders dominated the religious environment of Catholic homes. Devotion to saints and a focus on Mary proved powerful aspects within the formation

26. Edmund Arthur Moore, *A Catholic Runs for President: The Campaign of 1928* (New York: Ronald, 1956); Richard O'Connor, *The First Hurrah: A Biography of Alfred E. Smith* (New York: Putnam, 1970).

27. McGreevy, *Catholicism and American Freedom*, 151.

of Catholics at home. Author Madeleine Blaise (b. 1946) recalls that when her brother was born, "he was given the name Michael, and two middle names, Francis and Anthony, so two saints could watch over him. . . . To honor Michael's birth, a statue of Saint Francis was placed in the yard."[28] Saints became central characters in family life. The Virgin Mother was often at the front and center of this attention. For Claudia DeMonte, this presence became all too real for her: "One night I remember waking–I was seven or so–and thought I saw the Blessed Mother on the fire escape in our apartment building. . . . I mean, *Right from the Grotto with Bernadette to the fire escape.*"[29] Scholar Paula Kane notes that devotion to Mary experienced what she calls "its heyday in the mid-twentieth century" and ultimately declined after Vatican II. Such devotions took various forms, including parading images of Mary through the streets on feast days, hosting rosary nights in homes, and dedicating Tuesday evening to novenas in honor of the Virgin.[30] Honoring and treasuring this holy icon seemed to be a major element in almost every Catholic home.

The Blessed Virgin likely would have been one among many icons displayed by Catholic families. Most homes still contained evidence of the domestic ideology promoted in Victorian America only a few decades earlier. Parents–and grandparents, who had lived through the end of the nineteenth century–held onto the items and images that had brought religion into their intimate spaces. Such symbols would have included crucifixes, statues, holy pictures, and candles. These became commonplace objects and created an atmosphere of Catholic piety for the children who passed them regularly.

---

28. Madeleine Blais, *Uphill Walkers: Memoir of a Family* (New York: Atlantic Monthly Press, 2001), 20.

29. DeMonte, "The Whole World Was Italian," 58.

30. Paula Kane, "Marian Devotion since 1940: Continuity or Casualty?," in *Habits of Devotion*, 90.

*The Ethnic Neighborhood*

Between the public arena of the parish and the private domain of the home, one more space would have tremendous impact upon young Catholics: the neighborhood. This local community had its own way of establishing expectations and ingraining habits among the youth. Historian Mark Massa describes the "Catholic ghetto" as "a nurturing but confining subculture marked by membership in 'our' institutions from cradle to grave."[31] From the time one was born, a child was part of something larger and defining, even if she didn't realize its impact. Author Mary Gordon (b. 1949) looks back to explain the tangible, if unrecognized, effects of this during childhood: "Until I went to college I had no genuine contact with anyone who wasn't Catholic."[32] Once again, this type of insular environment would change by the end of the twentieth century with the demographic shifts on the horizon. Eventually scores of Catholics would begin moving away from these urban neighborhoods to settle in the more pluralistic suburbs. Even then, sometimes the move was simply a shift in place. Jay Dolan writes, "The parish of the immigrant neighborhood was transplanted to the American suburb."[33] So while remnants of this cocoon-like existence might still be felt in certain places, its overall disappearance contributes to the story of change in American Catholic experience across the decades.

During the 1940s, '50s, and '60s, the question "Where are you from?" would likely yield a response like "St. Patrick's" or "St. Anthony's" rather than any town or street name. It was the parish that defined one's origin. Once again, the settlement patterns of early

---

31. Mark Stephen Massa, *Catholics and American Culture: Fulton Sheen, Dorothy Day, and the Notre Dame Football Team* (New York: Crossroad, 1999), 2.

32. Mary Gordon, *Good Boys and Dead Girls: And Other Essays* (New York: Viking, 1991), 164.

33. Dolan, *American Catholic Experience*, 381.

immigrant Catholics would determine a significant character within the parish. With Catholic families usually settling together and ultimately organizing according to ethnic origins, enclaves among groups of Catholics from particular European countries emerged. One was not simply Catholic, one was Irish Catholic or Italian Catholic, for example. Their parish identity would reflect that and largely influence the nature of one's religious experience.

While exceptions existed and expanded as Catholicism grew in the United States, one could easily find herself surrounded by Irish Catholics, Italian Catholics, or Polish Catholics for most of her childhood during the mid-twentieth century. Claudia DeMonte's story provides an example. She narrates, "My family settled in an Italian neighborhood." This Italian character enveloped everything she knew as a child, even those aspects (and people) without the ethnic affiliation. She writes, "I grew up thinking that my mother was Italian. I mean, the whole world was Italian to me. My family was Italian and I had no idea my mother wasn't."[34] In this acknowledgment of her young naiveté, the artist reveals the power of the ethnic community that surrounded her. Before she knew the difference, it defined everything and everyone she knew.

Ethnic affiliation offered more than just identity; it established clear divisions among Catholics themselves. DeMonte remembers a particular tension with the local Irish Catholics that affected her and her classmates directly: "One time, in the sixth grade, we had a teacher who was Irish and gave the Italian kids extra homework. Then the next year we had an Italian teacher who gave the Irish kids extra homework."[35] Of course, DeMonte and her classmates were not the only ones to feel this tension. Conflict among ethnic groups had been a consistent problem among Catholics in

34. DeMonte, "Whole World Was Italian," 51.
35. Ibid., 56.

the United States since they began immigrating to this country. As immigrants moved to urban locations, they quickly discovered other groups from different places living nearby. They did not always get along. The particular tension alluded to by DeMonte between Italians and Irish Catholics was a common problem, and at the heart of it was religious difference. Robert Orsi succinctly sums it up: "Irish American Catholics could not understand Italian popular spirituality."[36] The mutual distrust between the two religious sensibilities requires a closer look at the historical context. For a variety of reasons, the Irish Americans claimed a significant portion of the Catholic clerics in the United States. They were strongly affiliated with the institutional church. Italian devotion to saints and their popular practice posed a direct challenge to the Irish hierarchy.[37] In his study *An Unlikely Union: The Love-Hate Story of New York's Irish and Italians*, Paul Moses explains, "There have always been dissenters, but in general, the Irish prized obedience to clerical authority and southern Italian immigrants were known to have an anticlerical streak."[38] This created and sustained tension between these two ethnic groups, but the youngsters were probably less concerned with the religious contexts than they were about the extra homework it meant for them. Later in life, if a mid-century Irish Catholic and an Italian Catholic were able to put such resentments behind them and fall in love, their lifelong union would be considered a "mixed marriage." As it turns out, this happened often. Moses notes, "They clashed in parishes, workplaces and politics. But over time, these arenas came to unite them." As a matter of fact, "the Irish and Italians eventually became two of the most

36. Robert A. Orsi, *The Madonna of 115th Street: Faith and Community in Italian Harlem, 1880–1950* (New Haven, Conn.: Yale University, 1985), 55.

37. See James Stuart Olson, *Catholic Immigrants in America* (Chicago: Nelson-Hall, 1987).

38. Paul Moses, *An Unlikely Union: The Love-Hate Story of New York's Irish and Italians* (New York: New York University Press, 2015), 29.

intermarried ethnic groups in America."[39] Early on, though, they felt removed and divided from one another.

Such insular ethnic environments could offer the benefit of safe havens and comfortable surroundings for their residents. As some writers note, however, there could be a downside to these close-knit neighborhoods. They could have the unwanted effect of imposing certain expectations and restrictions. Sometimes Irish and Italians even separately perceived similar limitations within their communities. Curiously, despite a rich intellectual tradition throughout Catholic history, many authors in this study communicate a kind of distrust of education passed along to them early in life. Mary Gordon claims, "I think that Irish love of learning was always tainted by the fear of learning. For the Irish, and for Catholics in general, learning, secular learning, is what will push you out of the fold."[40] Demonte's depiction resonates: "In the neighborhood I grew up in, the Italians were held back because of their attitude toward education. Education just wasn't that important to them. . . . The Italian kids who did go to college had unusual parents."[41] Despite the ethnic differences, these religious cultures bore similarities in the constraints some children may have internalized. The authors who went on to earn advanced degrees remember this element of their youth and ascribe it to a communal ethos.

One ethnic group that demands mention in its relationship to these stories is Latino/a Catholics, a label that applies broadly to people with a wide range of national origins with Spanish-speaking heritage. Well before the middle decades of the twentieth century, the focus of this study, and certainly since that time, Latino/a Catholicism has claimed a huge presence in the United States, with

39. Ibid., 4, 7.

40. Annie Lally Milhaven, "Mary Gordon," interview, in *Conversations with Mary Gordon*, ed. Alma Bennett (Jackson: University of Mississippi Press, 2002), 56.

41. DeMonte, "Whole World Was Italian," 56.

diverse stories of ethnic life among Catholic Americans. Their stories have begun to receive more scholarly attention in recent years, but, as that attention reveals, the deep history and influential future of these communities certainly demand more study in the years to come.[42] Because of the geographical origins of this book's sources, notably Northern and urban in most cases, the families with Spanish-speaking heritage considered here usually found themselves scattered among communities of otherwise European descendants and, for the most part, having to navigate their way through those circumstances. Authors claiming Hispanic identities, for example, share stories of dealing with Irish clergy in their churches and schools in New York City. In Sacramento, California, Richard Rodriguez learned English from the "Irish voices" that surrounded him—namely, the priests and nuns.[43] Removed as these experiences may have been from Latino/a communities elsewhere in the United States, their narratives contribute distinct perspectives on the cultural Catholicism studied here.

From imposing inevitable limitations to offering a wealth of opportunities for learning and living the faith, neighborhoods constituted a fundamental dimension to cultural Catholicism of the 1940s, '50s, and '60s. Close proximity allowed neighbors to share their own religious lessons with one another. Moreover, adults

42. For more on Latino/a Catholicism in the United States, see Mario T. Garcia, *Católicos: Resistance and Affirmation in Chicano Catholic History* (Austin: University of Texas Press, 2008); Timothy M. Matovina and Gary Riebe-Estrella, eds., *Horizons of the Sacred: Mexican Traditions in U.S. Catholicism* (Ithaca, N.Y.: Cornell University Press, 2002); Timothy M. Matovina, *Latino Catholicism: Transformation in America's Largest Church* (Princeton: Princeton University Press, 2011); Kristy Nabhan-Warren, "Hispanics and Religion in America," *Oxford Research Encyclopedia of Religion*, March 2016, http://religion.oxfordre.com/view/10.1093/acrefore/9780199340378.001.0001/acrefore-9780199340378-e-79, accessed January 6, 2017; Bishop Ricardo Ramirez, *Power from the Margins: The Emergence of the Latino in the Church and in Society* (Maryknoll, N.Y.: Orbis, 2016); Moises Sandoval, *On the Move: A History of the Hispanic Church in the United States*, 2nd ed. (Maryknoll, N.Y.: Orbis, 2006).

43. Richard Rodriguez, "The Fabric of Our Identity," interview by Krista Tippett, *On Being*, podcast, September 18, 2014.

could keep a close eye on kids to make sure everyone's children, not just their own, were being faithful Catholics.

## *Looking Back*

Three distinct settings, the parish/school, the home, and the neighborhood, comprised the Catholic world for mid-twentieth-century children. For many, these contexts blended into one integrated environment; for others, navigating through each of them would solicit particular behaviors and attitudes. Regardless, they were fundamentally linked. Garry Wills (b. 1934) identifies it as the "total weave of Catholic life" whereby a "single authority ran through each aspect of one's upbringing. That authority stood behind every practice, endorsing them all."[44] This chapter has laid out a general background for the nature of these settings. In the chapters that follow, literary depictions provide a glimpse into an American Catholic experience within them, distinct from what children encounter half a century later. These narrated representations have been carefully selected and crafted by their respective authors so that in these selections we gain access to the circumstances that mattered in writers' views of the past, or at least what they want shared. Their stories bring readers into the pews and classrooms, kitchens and bedrooms, and neighborhood stoops to offer firsthand reminiscences of the Catholic world they knew.

44. Garry Wills, "Memories of a Catholic Boyhood," in *Bare Ruined Choirs: Doubt, Prophesy and Radical Religion* (New York: Paulist Press), 21.

# CHAPTER 2

## Like an
## Owner's Manual for a
## Very Complicated
## Vehicle

⟲∞⟳

*Learning the Rules*
*in the Classroom and the*
*Confessional*

For Gina Cascone (b. 1955), the Lenten season initially offered a welcome respite from daily rosary recitation in her Catholic schoolroom. Once she realized that its ritual replacement, the Stations of the Cross, however, would involve unbearably long periods of kneeling, she yearned for the seated prayers to the Virgin. Cascone and some fellow female classmates devised a plan to withstand the challenge of these sessions. She explains,

There is a trick to being able to kneel that long to Sister's liking. After about five minutes, your back started to ache and after ten, your knees got numb. If you made any obvious movements to alleviate your discomfort, Sister (who was always watching) would poke you in the small of your back. . . . What you had to do was learn to move only the hips, which were well concealed under those pleated wool skirts. . . . Then, you work on the knees. . . .[1]

While ostensibly contemplating images inviting prayer—Jesus' suffering and death—students were contending with their own agony during the Stations of the Cross. While some may have offered up the discomfort to God, Cascone focused on alleviating it without getting caught. Either way, they prayed as instructed. In Cascone's depiction, hers was a realm of rituals and rules.

This anecdote provides a window onto the institutional Catholic world perceived by young people during the mid-twentieth century. The narrator's time is neatly marked by liturgical seasons; devotions dictate her days; women religious possess total authority; a prayer's posture and form precede theological meaning in young minds. Another text offers a helpful concept for unlocking the larger meaning of Cascone's story. David Plante's (b. 1940) protagonist in *The Catholic* claims, "My religion did not allow meaning outside itself, and in itself all its meanings were obvious."[2] The mid-twentieth-century Catholic environment provided a self-contained and self-supported world. Those individuals whose formative childhood years involved Catholic instruction, both at home and at school, suggest that little seemed to exist beyond the realm of Catholicism. Narrated accounts, both autobiographical and fictional, portray a broad spectrum of sentiment. By considering depictions across the range, this chapter aims to tap into the rich, concentrated world of Catholic parish life during the 1940s, '50s, and '60s.

For children, parish life took its most prominent forms in the way of religious instruction and first sacraments. Even those youngsters who did not attend Catholic school still experienced the church's pedagogy in weekly catechism class and preparation for

1. Gina Cascone, *Pagan Babies and Other Catholic Memories* (New York: St. Martin's Press, 1982), 122.
2. David Plante, *The Catholic*, 1st American ed. (New York: Atheneum, 1986), 91.

the sacraments. According to many narratives, the religious lessons, sacraments, and masses instilled young Catholics not only with the foundations and expressions of their faith, but also with what they understood as the best ways of being a Catholic. As adults reflect on their childhood experiences in these contexts, they highlight four ways in which the interactions had an impact: (1) high expectations were established by particular Catholic models; (2) rules and order assumed a central place in daily life; (3) lifelong unconscious habits took hold; and (4) sin and sacraments became everyday concepts with lasting consequence.

"My grammar school years especially were the years when the great Church doors opened to enclose me, filling my day as I was certain the Church filled all time," writes Richard Rodriguez (b. 1944).[3] Like many of the authors here, Rodriguez expresses the overwhelming experience of being enfolded by the Catholic Church as a child in parochial school. It took him in and became his frame of reference for understanding place and time. The characters within this environment loomed large for children. As suggested in the examples that follow, nuns and priests seemed to wield a power bestowed from above.

### Ideal Exemplars

Nuns and priests were set apart from all other Catholics. In dedicating themselves to a holy life in the church, these vowed women and men had answered God's call to serve. Such commitment commanded attention, even fascination. Mary Gordon writes about her memory of first seeing a nun at the age of three. The moment left an indelible impression: "Kneeling in the light falling on the pure blue of her habit, the whiteness of her hands, bouncing off her glasses, this nun knelt and showed me all I needed to know of per-

---

3. Richard Rodriguez, *Hunger of Memory: The Education of Richard Rodriguez; An Autobiography* (Boston: D. R. Godine, 1982), 80.

fect forms. . . . She was entirely still, and we were nothing to her; she was her function: a pray-er, one who prayed."[4]

Certainly, the three-year-old child perceiving this vision did not possess such descriptive language. Still, the observation had an unshakable effect, and the memory leads to this depiction decades later. The young child, barely more than a toddler, identified a holiness in what she saw. While she would not enter a Catholic schoolroom for a few years, clearly she had been prepared for this moment when a nun would become real for her. To be this riveted by such a scene, to sense a kind of embodied perfection, the young girl anticipated a high standard.

Gordon writes in another essay, "Women of God," that this high level of admiration later had practical implications throughout her youth: "For the whole of what I would call my childhood I wanted to be a nun."[5] She describes two of her favorite objects kept among her treasures: "my favorite book, *The Nuns Who Hurried*, and my favorite doll, a stiff coifed figure in a habit of dark silk." There were a few other nonreligious objects in this tiny collection, but she explains, "The nun doll and the nun book had a special shimmer. They made me feel exalted and apart."[6]

One would be hard-pressed today to encounter a three-year-old Catholic being so deeply moved by the initial observation, never mind aspiring throughout childhood to join the convent or treasuring a nun doll. Even in her day, while Mary Gordon's reaction might typify a kind of awe inspired by nuns, the totalizing captivation she expresses may have been much stronger than the norm. Still, the practical facts of nuns' diminishing numbers and the changes to their communities after Vatican II significantly limits

4. Mary Gordon, *Seeing through Places: Reflections on Geography and Identity* (New York: Scribner, 2000), 143.

5. Mary Gordon, "Women of God," *Atlantic*, January 2002, http://www.theatlantic.com/magazine/archive/2002/01/women-of-god/302377/, accessed January 14, 2015.

6. Ibid.

the potential for this scene in the twenty-first century. For Mary Gordon in the early 1950s, Sister provided an image of the ideal—indeed a difficult model to emulate and one that earned ultimate respect. As Gordon herself describes, once these women became human beings in her classrooms and later activists in her adulthood, her relationship to them shifts over time and becomes more complicated. Early on, however, they were simply a symbol of all that was holy and good.

Catherine Gildiner's (b. 1948) reflection on a nun provides a close look at one child's shifting understanding of an influential sister. She writes, "Mother Agnese still lives within me. She's been my most admirable role model and my most formidable foe."[7] Gildiner explains that from first grade through her teenage years, she was under the tutelage of Mother Agnese either as a teacher or principal. They both experienced significant transitions throughout this relationship. When the young girl first met the young woman, she was Sister Agnese and later Mother Agnese and eventually Mother Superior. Regarding her own phases, Gildiner explains, "I started as the good Catholic girl who wanted to be Mother Agnese for Halloween, trying desperately to emulate her holiness." Eventually, though, Gildiner would grow to become the self-described "angry teenager who went head-to-head with Mother Agnese, fighting for her emotional life." The author details many of their collaborations and confrontations, noting, "She always had the advantage, yet I was never given a handicap. She had God on her side and I was still trying to slide in on the right side of eternity, where she held the tickets to most of the seats."[8]

The classroom proved to be a site of contention between them, but the young girl was able to connect with Mother Agnese in another area: sports. In addition to serving as teacher and principal,

7. Catherine Gildiner, *Too Close to the Falls: A Memoir* (New York: Viking, 1999), 239.
8. Ibid., 240.

the nun also accepted the role of athletic director for the girls, not an uncommon practice for women who wore all sorts of hats in the schools they staffed. Catherine turned out to be a star athlete, competing ultimately for the state championship in the high jump. While Mother Agnese was coach, supporter, and ally in this process, she never let Catherine forget what was most important about it. When the young girl forgot to make the sign of the cross before an event during one of her meets, Mother Agnese reminded her she was "a Catholic ambassador" and she "must always try and make converts and show exemplary behavior in front of others."[9] This type of reprimand was not just for show, either. Gildiner writes, "Mother Agnese is the only person I ever met who never once stepped out of character. She lived and died a martyr." The teacher had little time or energy for "the usual minutiae of Catholic girlhood education," according to the author, and "always went right to life's marrow." This most frequently translated into her patented pedagogy, such as the custom of asking every first-grader at the beginning of the day what she would be sacrificing to help missionaries "convert souls in deepest, darkest Africa."[10]

These women established extraordinarily high standards, and their own personal example only exacerbated pressure—they had given up a future with a spouse and family. This detail received a great deal of attention from children who marveled at the nuns' wedding rings and veils, symbols of marriage to Christ. These intriguing features emphasized the sacrifice that accompanied their exemplary reverence. Martha Manning (b. 1952) explains that this also proved a site for inspiration: "As kids in Catholic school we always prayed for 'vocations.' . . . A 'true' vocation involved becoming a nun or a priest. Even the vocations of spouse and parent

9. Ibid., 268.
10. Ibid., 242.

were distant seconds to 'answering the call.'"[11] A certain moral superiority came with dedicating oneself to God, and so it was hoped by the church community that young Catholics might come to be called. Anne Rice offers even further reason for such widespread admiration: "It was understood that a dedicated, and celibate, nun or priest could come to understand things mystically that no non-virginal person could aspire to grasp."[12] Clearly, these women and men earned a place of respect through their chosen path.

Even moviegoers in the 1950s and '60s witnessed the ideal character of nuns on the big screen. In the 1959 film *The Nun's Story*, Audrey Hepburn's character, Gabrielle Van Der Mal, enters the convent to become Sr. Luke. The strict regulations and personal expectations Sr. Luke finds in the congregation intend to emulate nothing short of "perfect obedience as Christ practiced it." They demand humble behavior combined with complete purity—a range of practices from concealing one's hands to detaching oneself from memories of life before postulance. Sr. Luke learns from the beginning that holiness is both an internal and external state and its status was to be closely tracked. Twice each day for the rest of her life she must document all the ways that she has compromised her emulation of Christ's perfect obedience. "I accuse myself," each sister writes in her designated notebook, of such things as drinking a glass of water between meals without permission or speaking without necessity. The holy ideals of sacrifice and moral perfection come to life in this Hollywood depiction. In the end, Sr. Luke decides religious life had not been her true vocation and leaves the convent. While such a scandalous act might have surprised viewers, the conclusion seems only to confirm the demanding sacrifice of answering the call.

11. Martha Manning, *Chasing Grace: Reflections of a Catholic Girl, Grown Up* (San Francisco: HarperSanFrancisco, 1996), 131.

12. Rice, *Called Out of Darkness*, 50.

The literature of mid-twentieth-century Catholic childhoods features countless instances of model nuns who set the bar nearly out of reach. These women were students' primary contact with the institutional church and earned respect because of their personal sacrifice and reverent disposition, not to mention their command of the classroom. Their work, though, was to be overseen by the priests. Garry Wills recalls, "Priests, of course, were supposed to guide the nuns entrusted to their care—from the pulpit, in the confessional and as the schools' 'presidents.'"[13] For children, priests earned separate distinction for their authoritative position in the church and for their sacramental power. They were part of an apostolic legacy, both on and off the altar.

For someone like my own dad, who witnessed three of his mother's brothers answer the call to priesthood, the distinction of the office was on full display. The ordination events had an aura all their own. First the family would observe the grandeur of the sacramental ceremony itself, with the bishop at the center of the moment. Then would come the more personal encounter with their newest clergyman. Gathered at the home with close relatives and friends, they would await his arrival. Watching for the car to come around the corner, loved ones felt nervous anticipation to welcome their newly ordained to the celebration in his honor. He was no longer simply son, brother, or uncle; he was now a priest. The culmination of the events happened the next day when he would say his first Mass. As he made his way down the aisle to take his place upon the altar where he would consecrate the Eucharist, this young man accepted his place in a long line of men who had done the same. His importance and holiness could not be disputed.

Even those who couldn't boast a priest in the family still experienced the excitement that came with a priest's visit to their home. Richard Rodriguez recalls how such an occasion required special

13. Wills, "Memories of a Catholic Boyhood," 29.

preparations. He writes, "The first English-speaking dinner guest at our house was a priest from Sacred Heart Church . . . the visit was too important an event for me to forget. I remember how my mother dressed her four children in outfits it had taken her weeks to sew."[14] In their newest outfits and with their best manners, children figured out that priests were the most special of houseguests. From offering the special linen hand towels reserved for only the holiest of hands to scrubbing every inch of the house in the days leading up to the visit, Catholics welcomed priests with the closest thing they could to royal treatment.

Murray Bodo, OFM (b. 1937), writes, "I can't remember when I didn't want to be a priest." Reflecting on the sacrament of Holy Orders decades after receiving them himself, he describes the pretend masses he "said" as a child in his pretend vestments at his "play altar." He tries to imagine the appeal of such play to a young boy: "In a small New Mexico border town in the early 1940s, the priest at the altar must have seemed so special, so removed from the mundane, blue-collar lives of the coal miners and railroaders. . . . He was somehow elevated, different, worthy of emulation." This sense of status ultimately has no bearing on his later motivations to take vows. As a Franciscan priest, he says his work is "a ministry of working mercy with those who are or who perceive themselves as being on the margins, rejected, despised by others."[15] Still, this depiction of his childhood perception emphasizes the kind of star power priests seemed to exude. Author Monica Wood (b. 1954) recalls how her uncle's priesthood allowed her just a hint of stardom in the other corner of the country in a small town in Maine. She writes that during Father Bob's visits to her school, he makes no big show of addressing her or her sisters, giving them a knowing glance instead and, then, "roving

14. Rodriguez, *Hunger of Memory*, 82.

15. Murray Bodo, OFM, "Holy Orders," in *Signatures of Grace: Catholic Writers on the Sacraments*, ed. Thomas Grady and Paula Huston (New York: Dutton, 2000), 165, 188.

the room, singling out our friends instead of us, which is far more delicious, our glory deflecting to other kids who become celebrities once removed."[16] This grandeur, of course, was deeply rooted in the sacred position the priest occupied in the church. His place in a long line of Christ's servants and his ability to administer the sacraments accounted for this exalted standing. Though this nuanced importance might have been missed by children, they did understand that priests were special. Wood conveys a glimpse of that when she describes her own mother's relationship to that uncle. Writing about his youth, she explains, "They call him Bobby, until the moment of his ordination, when everyone, including his fourteen-years-older sister, will switch to 'Father Bob' in less time than it takes for him to transform wine into the blood of our Lord Jesus Christ."[17] The office held distinction; the distinction was to be recognized.

David Plante indicates that the perception of priests as special and powerful remains with him well into adulthood. He recalls total intimidation when his friend suggested they speak to the priest after a Mass they attended. He writes, "I had never been into the vestry. As devout as I'd been, I'd never been an altar boy and had never viewed Monsieur Cure as a man I could visit in the vestry after mass. I had never spoken to him outside of confession. I would have been as incapable of opening the door to the vestry . . . as I would have the tabernacle on the altar."[18] He highlights the extraordinary nature attributed to priests—inhabiting a different world that clearly set them apart and made them nearly as unapproachable as the Eucharist itself. It was a childhood lesson he didn't take lightly: before they were men, they were priests.

Mary Gordon offers another powerful example of the relation-

16. Monica Wood, *When We Were the Kennedys: A Memoir from Mexico, Maine* (New York: Houghton Mifflin, 2012), 56.

17. Ibid., 159.

18. David Plante, *American Ghosts* (Boston: Beacon, 2005), 222.

ship to priests. Regularly receiving the royal treatment upon their visits, announced or not, priests would regularly drop in on parish families to share a meal and engage in conversation. Gordon remembers frequent visits by her father's priest-friend to their family home. She recalls that the two men would often argue, her father yelling words like "orthodox" and "heresy," behind closed doors. What followed shocked her: "After they were through with their arguing, my father and Father B. would come out into the hall. And what happened then would alarm me more than anything. My father would fall to his knees and ask Father B. for his blessing. Father B. would place his hands on my father's head, whisper some Latin words, and make the sign of the cross above him."[19] She explains that her father recognized his own right to confront Father B. as a man, but that he always respected the office of the priesthood.

Through her narrative, Gordon communicates a powerful image of her father surrendering to the cleric. With their designated role in the church, their special language for religious matters, and their physical gestures that could bestow a blessing from God, priests commanded the respect and submission of Catholic men and women of all ages, social status, and piety. This narrated memory evidences the strong culture surrounding the relationship between clergy and laity. During the mid-twentieth century, children may not have grasped the concept of solemn vows or apostolic succession, but they sensed an aura among nuns and priests that put these adults on a higher level. Their roles and significance were part of a culture of meaning.

Today, priests and nuns are no less ordained or vowed, no less selfless or holy, no less devoted. So it could be asked: wouldn't this culture of meaning apply just as much today as it did fifty years ago? While the commitment on the part of priests and nuns has

19. Gordon, *Seeing through Places*, 153.

certainly not diminished, the circumstances surrounding their interactions and relationships with the laity have definitely changed. The fact that there are significantly fewer ordained priests and sisters means that many Catholics have a far smaller chance of personal encounters with these important church members. With so few priests serving so many Catholics, their responsibilities usually prevent them from visiting parishioners' homes for leisurely meals and intellectual discussion. Catholic teenagers are more likely to follow the pope's Twitter feed than to have a meal with their local pastor. Many Catholic schoolchildren will never be taught by a nun. Therefore, most young Catholics today will not experience that same holy aura simply because they will have much less chance to interact with priests and nuns.

For those who do have regular encounters with them, those encounters look and feel much different as a result of Vatican II. While the priestly ordination maintains the same connection to apostolic succession as it did in decades past, the elevated role of the laity has changed the dynamic. As a whole, lay individuals now have a stronger sense of their own voice and role in the church. Moreover, they actually participate much more directly with church governance and in ministry roles within their parishes. That level of participation, of course, does not diminish the holiness or centrality of priests, but it has yielded a change in the majority of Catholics' relationship to them. With regard to nuns, Vatican II had an enormous impact on their communities, and the effects of some of those deeply rooted changes would come to influence the perception of them among Catholics. On the surface, the very adjustment to their dress would have an impact. With the option to modify their habits, even abandon them altogether, many religious community members would come to look like any modest Catholic women. Their appearance no longer sets them apart. While it may seem minor, this does affect the way others perceive and relate to them. In most cases, it would be nearly impossible for my young daughter to identify a nun. This is a far cry from Mary Gordon's intense memory of seeing one for the first time at age three.

Technological advances have also had significant impacts among the laity, the clergy, and the nuns in the Catholic Church. The combination of the twenty-four-hour news cycle with social media and Internet forums has opened a new channel of communication between the church and its people. While Catholics might still be expected to go to Mass and participate in their parishes, they are no longer dependent on those local communities for accessing the church's global messages and teachings.

The perception of priests has also been dramatically affected by the recent sex abuse crisis. The devastating revelations of priestly abuse of minors throughout the past several decades have taken an enormous toll on the relationships between the laity and the ordained. Although the percentage of priests guilty of such atrocities and of bishops who did not reveal their crimes remains low, this tragedy in the church has certainly affected the public attitude toward the priestly office. For many, it has lost its aura, its power, its integrity. In fact, many have blamed that aura and sense of power for having contributed to this dire situation. The church has been reminded, in an all-too-terrible way, that these men are human, making them vulnerable to serious mistakes and sinfulness.

The church in the United States today is unequivocally different from that of the mid-twentieth century. Much has happened, for better and for worse. This has yielded tremendous change in the way the laity experience it. As we unpack the circumstances that characterized Catholic life in the 1940s, '50s, and '60s, we discover how much the nature of the relationships among priests, nuns, and the laity determined the character of that Catholic life. Returning to a time before the priestly office was so publicly marred, we encounter a realm of rules, ritual, and clear expectations.

## Rules, Order, and Consequences

Sr. Wilmette loomed large in my Catholic grade school during the 1980s, despite being the same height as most of the fourth-graders. Her notorious math lessons inspired fear in all of us, but it was her strict regulations for everything else that had most of us quaking. No one entered her classroom without a quick scan to ensure that his or her school uniform appeared to code and was clean. While all teachers required a proper heading at the top of every assignment—providing such information as the school, the teacher's and student's names, the date—Sr. Wilmette did not hesitate to give someone's math assignment a failing grade for a misplaced word in that section. Despite a day's worth of problems on the chalkboards lining the front of her room, by dismissal, the boards were once again pristine. Sr. Wilmette regularly made students wash them several times to get it just right. The children who might have had it the worst in her classroom, though, were those whose feet did not quite reach the floor when seated at their desks. Despite her own small stature, Sr. Wilmette issued an extra requirement to my shorter classmates. They needed to bring with them a tissue box upon which to rest their feet; dangling legs had no place in her classroom. We learned quickly that order mattered.

If the few nuns who still staffed my school imparted such lessons, it was even more serious business a few decades earlier. Justice Sonia Sotomayor (b. 1954) offers a succinct reflection on the characterizing feature of her Catholic education: "Discipline was what made Catholic school a good investment in my mother's eyes, worth the heavy burden of the tuition fees.... Among the black-bonneted nuns who managed classrooms of forty or fifty kids in my school, discipline was virtually an eighth sacrament."[20] The importance of

---

20. Sonia Sotomayor, *My Beloved World* (New York: Alfred A. Knopf, 2013), 30.

form and structure was part of every lesson, from handwriting to divine worship, and there was a definitive right way to do all things. In this chapter's opening example, Gina Cascone emphasized that a prayer's posture mattered, even if its discomfort may have proven distracting. In her memoir, Martha Manning details some of the specific ways that a culture of discipline and structure was created. She writes, "Second grade was . . . my first exposure to a particular kind of Catholic sin: nun sin. While pissing off a nun was not *technically* on any sin list, the displeasure and the consequences of transgressing one of the many rules within the nuns' classroom kingdom seemed much worse than any other kind of hell."[21] Manning invents a whole new category of sin, one that even seems to bypass God. According to her narratives, transgressing these teachers threatened an unappealing possibility comparable to eternal punishment. She recalls the daunting list of regulations: "Sister Jerome must have taken years to finesse her list of rules. They were pronounced as if she were reading from a tablet personally presented to her on Mount Sinai."[22] Students learned to follow the rules because their teachers and principals could so directly impact their lives, present and, it seemed, eternal.

Manning offers the especially poignant example of "the envelope commandment." This referred to her Sunday school teacher's rule that any absence required a note from the student's parents, with the note enclosed in a particular way. She explains, "It had to be in a letter-sized envelope. The envelope had to be unsealed. It could not have any writing on the front or back."[23] The author emphasizes the specificity of the rules, effectively portraying the nun as entirely inflexible. She describes the fear she felt the week she herself needed a note. Of course, her father had done it all wrong: "Instantly I

21. Manning, *Chasing Grace*, 36.
22. Ibid.
23. Ibid., 36–37.

knew it was unacceptable. It was in a legal-sized envelope. On the front he had written, 'Most Reverend Sister Miriam Jerome.' And, as if that weren't enough, it was sealed." That night, she recalls, "I stayed up all night in dread of Sunday school. It was the kind of dread for which there is no comfort."[24] Here, Manning depicts a Catholic world where the rules were clear, the stakes high, and the nuns in control. Recollecting the moment when she handed her father's note to the nun, however, Manning offers a new perspective on this religious woman. She recounts the instant she turned in the envelope: "She was flushed and I was sure I was dead meat. But then she beamed. 'Please thank your father for the lovely note,' she said, motioning for me to take my seat. . . . In that small space of time, she lost her pug face and her threatening stance. She looked softer somehow, almost human."[25] Manning remembers being stunned by this response. She describes becoming aware that a human being lived within the habit. As a child, this realization came only at choice moments and would not last long. Such a limited worldview prevented her, at the time, from grasping fully what had just transpired. It had never occurred to her that the strict envelope commandment was a creative way for the nuns, who had few resources, to acquire paper for their personal use. Neither had it occurred to her that despite doing the most work, these women received minimal appreciation. She writes, "I didn't understand that my father's respectful acknowledgment of 'Most Reverend Sister Miriam Jerome' would be worth far more to her than any virginal envelope."[26] Rules were rules. There was a right way and wrong way to do just about anything in Manning's Sunday school world. As it turned out, sometimes there was pragmatic justification for such strictness, and in rare times such rules could even be broken.

24. Ibid., 37.
25. Ibid.
26. Ibid., 38.

We see such rule-breaking exception take on life in the popular 1945 film *Bells of St. Mary's* after parish school teacher Sr. Benedict, played by Ingrid Bergman, witnesses one student being bullied and beat up by another. When the new pastor, Fr. O'Malley, playfully congratulates young Tommy for winning the fight against Eddie, Sr. Benedict reminds the priest, played by Bing Crosby, that they "don't tolerate fighting." The energetic pastor encourages educating the youth before expelling him, and the seasoned teacher cautions against showing pride for the boy's fighting ability. Ultimately, Sr. Benedict decides to bend the rules when she takes it upon herself, with the aid of the book *The Art of Boxing*, to teach young Eddie how to defend himself against Tommy. As the habited nun shows her student the importance of the bob-and-weave and the one-two punch, Sr. Benedict reveals that rule-breaking was possible, even if not expected. When these lessons are tested outside her classroom window, viewers watch her shadow-box along with her protégé, visibly taking pleasure in his success in the contest. She was, in fact, human. For children growing up in the reality of Catholic schooling, predicting such occasions was an impossible feat, so falling into line was the unquestionably wise practice.

Rules, discipline, and structure do seem to reign supreme among these narratives. While practical needs might account for an occasional classroom commandment, as in Manning's example, author Monica Wood offers another reflection that proves helpful in understanding this climate. She writes, "The Catholic tradition of my childhood—which I recall with affection, some awe, and a measure of yearning—did not allow for randomness. Every word and deed, every sorrow and triumph, every birth and death belonged to a Divine Plan."[27] Wood's awareness applies mostly to one's larger lot in life, and ultimately the comfort that could be felt in knowing it was

27. Wood, *When We Were the Kennedys*, 160.

all part of God's intentional—and beautiful—plan. Still, this perception of the higher purpose behind all human things seemed to trickle down into the more mundane details. Order and form mattered greatly; there was no place for randomness or disorder. Literature on the topic shows that classroom routines and sacramental preparations offered two opportunities for nuns to impart these important lessons.

Usually such order began with the actual structure of a school day. In most cases, its transitions were marked by prayer. School would begin with the Morning Offering. Before recess, children would call upon their personal helpers in the Prayer to My Guardian Angel. The Angelus would acknowledge the strike of noon. After lunch, students might say the Creed and then the day would be completed with an Act of Contrition. It was orderly and precise. Alice McDermott indicates that this sense of structure was a defining aspect of her early education. In the process of searching for a school for her son, she takes a self-tour of a Catholic school as an adult. She writes, "It was all too familiar: the uniforms, the orderly rows of desks, the crucifixes and holy water fonts and carefully colored cutouts of little lambs and big-eyed shepherd children." In these small details, she feels immediately pulled back to her own Catholic grammar school and recalls how "Sr. Edwina stalked the place like a long-robed Captain Bligh."[28] Her narration includes a humorously exaggerated sense of anxiety provoked by this visceral memory, but the tone emphasizes the strict focus on order she so vividly remembers.

In her reflection on the nuns' approach to pedagogy, Madeleine Blais suggests, "The main disciplinary strategy was to treat misdemeanors as if they were felonies. You earned demerits if your nylons sagged or had runs: a messy outer life announced an equal-

28. Alice McDermott, "The Lunatic in the Pew," in *The Best Catholic Writing 2004*, ed. Brian Doyle (Chicago: Loyola Press, 2004), 2.

ly sloppy inner one."[29] Even in one's self-presentation and dress, one's moral code comes into play because it clearly reflected one's character.

Edward Rivera (1939–2001) also recalls learning correct ways of doing just about everything. He notes the reprimands students would face for certain actions categorized as "sinning" and details such offenses: "Meaning you hadn't done your homework by Catholic standards, or had talked out of turn in class, in fact almost anything they decided wasn't 'right' or—as Sister Mary McCollough, our principal, used to put it, with her eyebrows bunched up and her lips pursed—anything that did not 'redound to the greater honor and glory of the Holy Mother.' Holy Mother was always *Church*."[30] The standards seemed unreachably high, but there was no other choice. One aimed to follow directions or faced the consequences. Curiously, an encounter well beyond school property reveals that despite his bitterness, Rivera learned to respect the nuns and their authority. When First Communion time was approaching and some of the children did not own the proper attire, Sr. Felicia took them to buy new clothes. Rivera describes his sense of surprise at this about-face from chastisement to generosity: "The whole bunch of us had a lot to learn about these women, and a lot to be grateful for as well. Not that we had much choice, but still. . . ."[31] Like Manning, Rivera indicates that the nuns were capable of surprises, and such surprises could evoke an awareness of their humanity. Then, he describes the urge to maintain the nun's authority, even if it had caused him problems at school. He describes Sister's conversation with the salesperson, and when the salesperson tries to mock the nun, the young boy is drawn to defend her. Rivera writes,

29. Blais, *Uphill Walkers*, 124.
30. Edward Rivera, *Family Installments: Memories of Growing Up Hispanic* (New York: Penguin, 1983), 74.
31. Ibid., 78.

"I didn't like people pulling our nuns' legs, and pretended not to understand his prank."[32] Surprisingly, when presented with the opportunity to get back at his strict teacher, he elects to protect her authority. When someone from the outside challenges the dynamics inside the Catholic world, this youngster comes to defend what he has internalized as the proper conduct within his realm of rules.

Sacramental preparation proved an important site, both for students' learning the importance of form and for nuns' instilling a sense of discipline. John Bernard Ruane (b. 1957) recalls his own in 1964. His class would be the first to make its First Holy Communion in the newly built parish church. The stakes were high. Ruane narrates an early practice session. His teacher Sister Mary made the plan perfectly clear: "'Now, as we proceed to the altar, it is very important that we do it in a very honorable and dignified fashion,' this intense nun said, determined to make this the most organized First Communion ceremony in the history of the Roman Catholic Church." As if that weren't pressure enough, the author describes the personal burden he felt. Sister Mary continues: "'Mr. Ruane and Miss Donnelly, you are first, so you have an important responsibility here. If you start the procession correctly, we will have a beautiful ceremony. If not, it will be a disaster. Do you understand?'"[33] Sr. Mary clearly meant business, and the young communicants accepted the task. The momentous occasion of one's First Holy Communion marked a critical experience in the life of a Catholic. One way for the nuns to impart the gravity of this transition was to emphasize the importance of form and structure. Even if they had no idea what they were actually doing there, students figured out that it was important. This literature is filled with First Communion anecdotes—the special outfits, the unprecedented attention, and the

32. Ibid., 83.
33. John Bernard Ruane, *Parish the Thought: An Inspirational Memoir of Growing Up Catholic in the 1960s* (Roswell, Ga.: Roswell Press, 2007), 17.

requisite celebrations. Behind these colorful descriptions lie the imparted lessons of careful preparation and orderly execution. Later in this chapter, I will consider some of the theological confusion posed by this life-changing moment. Despite any religious misperceptions, children grasped the gravity of a well-organized production.

Discipline, rules, and authority have been key ingredients in the preceding anecdotes from the Catholic world of the mid-twentieth century among youths. Enforced by the nuns and priests, regulations prescribed behavior and activity in Catholic schools. It becomes easy to see how discipline could become so closely connected to notions of faith and religious practice and how faith and religious practice became interwoven into everyday life. That seemingly ubiquitous process would have long-lasting consequence.

### Die-Hard Habits

Rules were not the only Catholic elements internalized by young students of the faith. Reflexive thoughts, prayers, and postures settled into psyches and bodies of Catholics, regularly surfacing regardless of distance from early religious environments. Writers indicate that certain aspects of religious language and movement were so pervasive during their childhoods that they produced long-lasting habits that forever connect them to that Catholic past.

One such defining element was *The Baltimore Catechism*. One would be hard-pressed to find a Catholic who grew up during the mid-twentieth century in the United States and did not know this volume well. Indeed, for most, it was *the* introductory document for the beliefs they would hold as lifelong Catholics. It was issued in the United States in 1885 and revised in 1941. There were four parts, and each part was structured in a question-and-answer format, making it particularly accessible for educational purposes. Authors describe regular recitation of this religious instruction. Patricia Hampl (b. 1946) suggests that the ritual question-and-answer sessions could even prove seductive. She writes, "The sky-blue Baltimore Catechism, small and square, read like an owner's manual for a very complicated vehicle. There was something pleasant, lulling, rhythmic, like heavily rhymed poetry, about the singsong Q-and-A format. Who would not give over heart, if not mind, to the brisk assurance of the Baltimore prose. . . ."[34] The ritual repetition of the catechism became something familiar and easy as these children were growing up. Its rhythm and reliability were a fixed part of religious instruction. Further, *The Baltimore Catechism* put the world into simple and clear terms. Designated questions and satisfactory answers laid out the young Catholic's place in the world. There was little room for doubt. For example, one question asked, "Who made the world?" and would be answered, "God made the world." To follow this up, "Who is God?" and the response: "God is the creator of heaven and earth and of all things." If there was any question where the young Catholic herself fell into this scheme, that concern was addressed. The question: "Why did God make you?" and the answer: "God made me to know Him, to love Him, and to serve Him in this world, and to be happy with Him forever in the next."[35] Life was clearly spelled out and made perfectly knowable to the extent that it needed to be known. There was little reason to think that anything lay outside that neat, comforting structure that contained full authority.

For my father and his adolescent classmates, one's mastery of the catechism's Q&A brought with it especially high stakes upon the occasion of their confirmation. Administered by the bishop, this sacrament brought the parish and its members under serious scrutiny. The young Catholics who were accepting full responsibility of

34. Patricia Hampl, *Virgin Time: In Search of the Contemplative Life* (New York: Ballantine, 1993), 47.
35. Michael A. McGuire, *Father McGuire's the New Baltimore Catechism*, official rev. ed. (New York: Benziger Brothers, 1942).

their chosen faith had to prove their comprehensive knowledge of the catechism. This could be demonstrated during the quiz portion of the ceremony when any confirmand could be called upon to answer any question from the authoritative book. My dad remembers that the reputation of the parish rested on each precise response. Solid preparation and steel nerves were the name of the game.

In her essay "I Am Catholic," first published in her *New York Times* column, Anna Quindlen (b. 1952) discusses her religious upbringing and concurs that one's ability to answer the questions was the primary concern. She writes, "I could recite parts of the Baltimore Catechism in my sleep. Do I believe those words? I don't know."[36] Proof of one's firm commitment to the questions' answers apparently was not a requirement. What mattered was only that the responses were committed to memory, that they became part of one's unquestioned makeup. The rest could be presumed. Such rote memorization was a key tool for teaching during those decades across the curriculum, but the Catholic Q&A seems to have established firm anchors in young students' minds. *The Baltimore Catechism* would be replaced in 1994 by the *Catechism of the Catholic Church* after decades of work by bishops to renew the teaching of the faith in light of the Second Vatican Council. Much less accessible to lay readers, never mind children, and intended for clergy and catechism teachers, the *Catechism of the Catholic Church* would not replicate the familiar and memorable character of *The Baltimore Catechism*.

In addition to the questions and answers of *The Baltimore Catechism*, authors identify other refrains from their Catholic educations that creep up at the most unexpected times. Even when one is securely situated in a secular environment, the pervasive religious upbringing surfaces in everyday experiences. In her novel *A Bigamist's Daughter*, Alice McDermott's introduction to the protagonist

36. Quindlen, *Living Out Loud*, 158.

features her on the phone, scribbling notes. In the first few pages of the novel, "Elizabeth writes, 'This is the day that the Lord hath made.'. . . She hangs up the phone and stares at the paper. Remnants of Catholic brainwashing or God trying to get a message to her?"[37] One of the many phrases learned in Catholic grade school provides the first characterization of this woman. The description exemplifies habits that emerge from mid-twentieth-century Catholicism. Elizabeth's pious expression in her doodling seems to be an unconscious manifestation of the lessons learned decades earlier. It happens often to this character. In another scene where she and her lover are walking through a park, Elizabeth expresses disappointment when her companion does not recognize any title of the movies she knows to have been filmed at that spot. The meaningfulness of the moment is lost. She makes a comparison in her mind: "Like watching the sunset with an atheist. She thinks of telling him this but fears the tangle of logic behind it; fears it's an expression she learned from the nuns."[38] Author McDermott draws this character with a certain inability to distinguish her own thoughts from the innumerable phrases she internalized during elementary school. The impulse to compare this secular experience in the park to one involving religious belief comes naturally to Elizabeth. Cultural Catholicism provided a lens for all aspects of life; authors indicate that seeing the world through such a lens is a hard habit to break.

Like McDermott, Rita Ciresi (b. 1960) also deploys automatic responses betraying a Catholic education to characterize her protagonist. Lise, from the novel *Pink Slip*, reacts to authority and perceives certain situations in a way that suggests a childhood marked by cultural Catholicism. For example, in one instance when an important person arrives to a work meeting, the narrator explains,

37. Alice McDermott, *A Bigamist's Daughter: A Novel* (New York: Random House, 1982), 6.
38. Ibid., 111.

"I bolted up from my chair as if the priest had entered the room during catechism assembly and the nuns had commanded: 'Stand for Father!'"[39] Indeed, the authority of nuns and priests and the reverence with which children were taught to address them made a serious impression on this character. It has caused her to perceive most contexts of authority in ways similarly to those of her childhood. At still another meeting, she describes its conclusion: "Peggy nodded and pronounced the meeting adjourned—a command that had the same effect as a priest saying, 'Mass has ended. Go in peace.'"[40] Ciresi draws her character to show how Lise's perspective has been so shaped by the experience of growing up in a Catholic environment that she seems to make sense of events according to its terms. The author represents an upbringing so inundated with Catholic authority and ritual that religious experience becomes a filter for perceiving secular adult life. Regardless of whether she believes, the character's Catholic childhood has shaped her and her understanding of the world.

In another automatic response, John Grogan narrates his mental and physical reaction to the news of his father's impending death: "I did something I had not done for many, many years. I prayed. I began just as I had started my prayers each night as a young boy. 'Dear Jesus, dear God the Father, dear Holy Spirit, all the saints and angels in Heaven.'. . . I made the sign of the cross just as the nuns had taught me four decades earlier."[41] Faced with terrible circumstances, Grogan finds himself turning to a familiar place of hope and comfort. While he might not have practiced, or even believed, since he was young, the habit of prayer from his childhood rushes back to him in a moment of helplessness.

Scholar Robert Orsi sheds some light on these ingrained re-

39. Rita Ciresi, *Pink Slip* (New York: Delacorte, 1999), 248.
40. Ibid., 257.
41. Grogan, *Longest Trip Home*, 285.

sponses in his work on Catholic life during the mid-twentieth-century *Between Heaven and Earth*. He might even argue that these types of mindless reactions were exactly the goal of some early religious formation. He writes, "Catholic children were encouraged to pray constantly—aloud with their classmates at regular times, at home before meals and at bedtime, silently as they sat at their desks, when they walked home in the afternoons, or while they played." They learned that such prayers could have consequences for those both dead (in purgatory, for example) and alive. With the potential of such powerful effects, prayer became more appealing for children who wanted to contribute in some way. This push toward constant prayer was accompanied by other ways of externalizing Catholics' faith and practice, particularly through postures or physical expression. Orsi concludes that adult Catholics, concerned about their place in American society, "worked fervently to render the interiority of Catholic faith visible and materially substantive for children—and for themselves."[42] So, the inclination to stand for Father or turn to prayer in times of need had deep roots in these efforts, which simply constituted ordinary life for many Catholic children of the time.

Even years later, the next generation of Catholics, with their faith firmly established in American society, experienced the imparted goal of making prayer and devotion public. My siblings and I have distinct memories of these efforts. My sister recalls the practice of constructing spiritual bouquets on special occasions during grade school. Children would be encouraged to say prayers for a special intention and keep track of the number said. The sum of everyone's prayers would then be totaled and marked down with the drawing of flowers and presented to the recipient. Msgr. O'Brien, the pastor, could boast quite a collection. My faith

42. Orsi, *Between Heaven and Earth*, 108–9.

and that of my basketball teammates was on regular display during our season. Blessing oneself at the foul line was a no-brainer part of everyone's free-throw routine, and when we faced major competition, passers-by might notice us ducking into church for a quick round of Stations of the Cross before school on game day. A less noticeable detail, if worn properly, was the scapular that just about every team member concealed under her uniform. These thin wool necklaces with postage-stamp–size images of saints on the front and back were intended to bring us strength when we hit the court. I am certain none of us knew their ancient origins as part of the monastic habit; we just knew it made us part of something and offered a good connection to God who might help against formidable opponents. We had inherited lessons about the power of prayer in all circumstances. We were not afraid to use it for causes big and small. It is easy to see how prayer as habit was a natural consequence.

### The Soul and the Sacraments

When she was five years old, my daughter informed me that she knew about some "very, very bad words." I had understood elementary school could impart less-than-desirable additions to her known vocabulary, so I braced myself when she asked, "Do you know what they are?" I was curious. Horrified and slightly embarrassed, she whispered, "Dead, kill, and gun." Relieved (and still a little saddened by the reality of the world's ever-present violence), I reassured her that these were bad words. Then she said, "But do you know what the worst word is?" Still a little uneasy about the possibilities, I shook my head. "Hell," she asserted and went on to say that was a place for "really, really" (which went on for several "really's") bad people. After that confident statement, however, her certainty wavered, and she wondered, "Is hell a real place?" At this point, any formal theological or religious training I have had went out the window. I had to answer the only way I knew, and I told her the truth: "I don't know. Some people think it might, but no one really knows for sure." It was the best I could do. She appeared a bit unsatisfied, but didn't press it. Quickly, as five-year-olds do, she moved onto something new.

The interaction struck me deeply, not simply because my young daughter was asking profound questions, but because the answer she received from me would differ so remarkably from the answer my parents might have been given to that same question during their childhood. For American Catholics of the 1940s, '50s, and '60s, hell was as real a place as any. It loomed large and posed a scary threat to the fate of one's soul, no matter how young or old. Hell may similarly have been a bad word among my parents' kindergarten classmates, but there was no question about its existence or its importance in one's own life. It was the alternative to heaven that was to be avoided at all costs.

Authors depicting Catholic experience during the mid-twentieth century feature this reality prominently in their work. The tone varies—some poke fun at the grave moral concerns experienced by seven-year-olds and others describe serious anxiety produced by a focus on the soul's eternal future—but it is a nearly ubiquitous topic one way or another. A look into the autobiographical and fictional depictions of that concern offers invaluable access into the Catholic culture of the time.

In an interview with Mary Gordon about her writing career, the interrogating journalist notes that Gordon's "natural subject became the secrets of the Catholic world" and wondered exactly what kind of secrets were included. Gordon answers, "I think that there was a secret language, and that language created categories of thought." She continues her characterization of this world: "At the center of it, for many Catholics, there was an enormously serious issue, which is, how do you become a saint? How do you save your soul? And that shaped everything in a way that was very unlike other religious traditions."[43] For children growing up in this Catholic environment, the preoccupation with one's soul seamlessly slipped into more routine concerns. From home to school to church and everywhere in between, there was an ever-looming awareness of how one's actions *and* thoughts could have an impact on one's current moral standing. No one would have been inquiring about the nature, never mind existence, of hell; instead children might be assessing their likelihood of ending up there.

In his short story "Baseball Fever," Tony Ardizzone (b. 1949) captures this childhood worry through the experience of his seven-year-old narrator, Daniel Paradiso. When a traumatic, life-altering event happens to young Daniel, his entire frame of reference for interpreting the incident relates to his notions of sin, soul, and hell. Ardizzone opens the story with a description of the narrator's earliest educators: "The Sisters of Christian Charity, to whom I was delivered at age six by my well-meaning parents for instruction and the salvation of my eternal soul."[44] Lessons featured the three possibilities for afterlife: "Heaven, Hell, or Purgatory—no substitutions."[45] At first, this did not seem too threatening. With such advance warning, they could closely monitor every action to avoid the worst option. Unfortunately, though, it was not so easy. Daniel narrates, "Because, the nuns informed us, even though we were barely able to cross Clark Street with the aid of a green light and two patrol boys, all of us had *already earned* Hell's hottest flames, all because of two people we hadn't even met."[46] Through discussions of Adam and Eve, the children began to learn that evil lurked everywhere. It was their task to avoid the fallen angels who were "hoping to lead

43. Eleanor Wachtel, "Mary Gordon," interview, in *Conversations with Mary Gordon*, 85.

44. Tony Ardizzone, "Baseball Fever," in *Taking It Home: Stories from the Neighborhood* (Urbana: University of Illinois Press, 1996), 1.

45. Ibid., 3.

46. Ibid.

(them) into the darkness of despair, into temptation, occasions of sin, eternal everlasting damnation."[47] This dramatic portrayal of their daily challenge sets the scene for the moment that changes things forever. In a routine game of neighborhood baseball, the kind that happens all the time in their Chicago back alley, Daniel finds himself up to bat with Mickey Meenan, an anomaly for being a Catholic only child, playing first base. Daniel feels the ball leave the bat in a line drive that hits Mickey right in the throat, the Adam's apple, no less. This terrible accident would kill Mickey, and the young batter had to face his horrific sin of murder. That night, his mother did not kiss him goodnight because, he decides, "my forehead now had the mark of Cain, and even in the darkness my own mother could see it." He ends up running away the next day, only to spend the whole time on the El train and return by dinner. In the meantime, though, he catches scarlet fever and finds himself frightfully ill. Burning up from the virus, he thinks a lot about hell: "I'd let my fever work itself up until I felt I was made of fire, and then I'd squint at the endless rows of candles. . . . I'd pretend it was a glimpse of Hell."[48] Ultimately, Daniel does bounce back physically, but psychologically and spiritually, he faces a long recovery. Ardizzone's short story obviously sensationalizes the details of young Daniel's experience. His reader feels pulled into the dramatic perception of the boy's dark nights of the soul. The embellished description in this fictional tale intentionally emphasizes the centrality of the soul for children raised Catholic in mid-twentieth-century America. It seemed most of life was premised on making heaven a possibility, or at least doing whatever one could to avoid hell.

Not surprisingly, clear instructions from knowing adults would specify to children the best way of pursuing their eternal goals—

47. Ibid., 6.
48. Ibid., 15–16.

namely, avoiding sin and receiving grace through the sacraments. First confession and First Communion, then, took on enormous importance in the elementary school years. Through preparation for these two rites of passage, children would come face to face with the crux of their faith, and in some cases more habits would take hold as a result. Again, the literary depictions of such encounters range from light-hearted nostalgia to deep theological reflection. What emerges consistently, though, is the prevalence and significance of these two sacraments. Both autobiographical and fictional accounts contain poignant moments ranging from sincere concern to utter confusion to tremendous satisfaction.

At seven years old, young Catholics became eligible (and required) to have their first confession. It demanded significant preparation: an understanding of the concept of sin, memorization of the prayers, a repenting heart. Even though they could not claim much life experience by this time, the responsibility that came with turning seven was something for which they had been prepared. Just as nuns and priests depicted in this literature made it clear which actions were acceptable for the classroom and the pew, they also reminded students which actions would make them worthy of salvation and, of course, those that would automatically exclude them from it. The bad news, according to the literature, was that a salvation-worthy lifestyle usually precluded all of the most tempting behavior, even deeds that might otherwise seem mundane. The good news was that one could always erase any sinfulness from the slate by means of confession.

As these students were learning what it meant to be human beings, they were made well aware of the pitfalls of sin that came with their existential state. From what they could tell, there was simply no way to avoid it. If evading sin was out of the question, then, young Catholics figured out that they had every reason to make the best confession they could so they might be forgiven these inevitable sins and have a chance at heaven. This meant, naturally, that they had to know just what constituted a sin so they could confess it properly. This task proved to be the first challenge, as Martha Manning notes: "Second grade marked the beginning of years of what-if questions posed to priests and nuns for the purpose of testing the absolute boundaries of sin." By compiling hypothetical situations for potential sin (for example, touching oneself "down there" but only to scratch an itch) and presenting them to the experts on the topic, priests and nuns, these children worked on developing their own expertise on sin.[49] In Manning's portrayal, this effort to recognize sin becomes something of an obsession among these anxious students. At the same time, complete comprehension was certainly not a prerequisite for confessing. In fact, Manning recalls her own first confession and the moment she accepted responsibility for her sins by listing them and their frequency: "Disobeyed my parents—eight times; fought with my brothers and sisters—six times; used a swear word—one time; lied—two times; committed adultery—four times." She would be interrupted by her confessor: "'What?' he bellowed, loud enough for everyone outside to hear him. '*What* did you do?'"[50] A brief conversation would clarify that the seven-year-old was not actually eligible for the sin of adultery. With a mix of naiveté and determination, the young Manning had wanted to ensure she had covered all her bases and made the most thorough confession possible. The humorous anecdote reveals the gravity with which children accepted the task of assessing their sinfulness, as well as the inability to grasp fully just what that might include.

With the sacrament of confession (known better as reconciliation today) currently waning among American Catholics, the generation before me recalls the powerful pull to the confession-

49. Manning, *Chasing Grace*, 35.
50. Ibid., 41.

al fueled by the hope of staying in God's good graces. One strong memory would be the long lines winding out of churches during the historical period known as the Cuban Missile Crisis. During a thirteen-day stand-off between the Soviet Union and the United States over nuclear arms the Soviet Union had placed in nearby Cuba, Americans legitimately feared onset of the next world war and therefore did what they could to prepare for death and the afterlife. For Catholics, that meant confessing one's sins as often as necessary. Scholar Peter Gilmour describes the scene: "During the Cuban Missile Crisis, Catholics lined the aisles of churches and chapels to go to Confession. Some lines snaked along the sidewalks around these houses of God."[51] This powerful image left its mark. In both autobiographical and fictional writing, authors highlight how this lesson was internalized even without the threat of war looming. High stakes meant they could not risk dying without confessing. Mary Gordon recalls a summer Saturday afternoon during adolescence when she went to church for confession, "knowing (she) was in a state of mortal sin." When she realized she would not have her pick of confessors and would have to go to Father W., she remembers, "I was sickened by my lack of choice." As she narrates, though, she could not let potential embarrassment before this priest, a family friend, impede her receiving the sacrament. She writes, "To go on longer than I had to in a state of mortal sin because of something so paltry as psychological discomfort would have been a serious error, perhaps even sinful in itself."[52] Gordon's description of the crucial moment emphasizes an intense motivation within this young Catholic. She suggests that she learned to evaluate her actions and thoughts constantly so that she would know when she needed to confess. It became almost second nature.

51. Peter Gilmour, "Spiritual Shifts (Odds and Ends)," *U.S. Catholic Magazine* 67, no. 1 (2002).
52. Gordon, *Seeing through Places*, 175.

With such intense "scrupulosity," a term that children would learn to associate with scouring one's soul for sin, came an intense sense of relief provided through the sacrament. A ready solution to the problem of sinfulness, confession offered a tremendous release for those suffering with their moral states. Its predictable process and outcome had tremendous appeal. Richard Rodriguez recalls its formulaic ritual and the absolution it yielded. He remembers the way the prayer begins, "Bless me, father, for I have sinned . . ." and the routine list of transgressions (such as "disobeyed my parents fourteen times") so often repeated. Rodriguez notes the end result: "I was forgiven each time I sought forgiveness. The priest murmured Latin words of forgiveness in the confessional box. And I would leave the dark."[53] For Rodriguez, it was habitual and familiar but also transforming each time it was experienced.

In Rita Ciresi's novel *Pink Slip*, her narrator Lise longs for that simple solution she enjoyed as a child. Upon leaving confession as an adult, the narrator laments, "I remembered how easy it all seemed back in the days of catechism, marching into the confessional and admitting I had told a few lies and said an occasional *shit* or *damn*. Then I had slipped up to the altar and recited my three Hail Marys and two Our Fathers, leaving the church feeling utterly free and pure, as if the pressing weight of the cross itself had been lifted off my shoulders."[54]

It might have seemed daunting at first, but as writers describe it, once the ritual was mastered and the prayers memorized, penance had enormous potential for these young practitioners. The promise of being pardoned became a long-attractive possibility within this Catholic world. Indeed, the consequences of certain actions had been made crystal-clear to Catholic children, not only for this life but also for the next. It brought peace of mind to think

53. Rodriguez, *Hunger of Memory*, 85.
54. Ciresi, *Pink Slip*, 57.

that penance would produce a more favorable consequence than unforgiven sin.

Once children received their first confession, it quickly fit into their normal routines. Alice McDermott includes confession among the regular family rituals that filled her childhood. She writes, "My family attended ten o'clock Mass every Sunday without fail, confession once a month on Saturday if the nuns hadn't taken care of it at school (or if our behavior required additional penance)."[55] Her narration communicated a sort of inevitability of confession, an expected part of week-to-week life. Notably, her conditions for attending confession on Saturday indicate that her moral state required close monitoring—either the nuns had not arranged for the sacrament at school *or* there had been enough sinning to require extra confessing. In either case, it necessitated an awareness of one's need for sacramental forgiveness. Patricia Hampl offers a scene even beyond the pressures of family life. She writes of the 1950s and '60s, "On a Saturday night, this typical exchange: someone, probably my brother, calling out, 'Wanna go to the movie at the Uptown?' And one of us replies, 'Sure. Go to confession first? Movie doesn't start till 7:30.' The easy presence of sacramental life all around us."[56] I suspect that anyone who grew up in this kind of Catholic environment would read that depiction and knowingly nod along with memories of their own nearly identical exchanges. On the other hand, if I were to ask a collection of Catholic teenagers today if that sounds familiar, I am certain I would get several blank stares, maybe worse. For a variety of reasons, the instinctive connection between Saturday afternoons and the sacrament of confession has all but disappeared among today's Catholic young people.[57] While

55. Alice McDermott, "Confessions of a Reluctant Catholic," 12.

56. Hampl, "Penance," in *Signatures of Grace*, 34.

57. For a history of confession throughout twentieth-century United States, see O'Toole, "In the Court of Conscience: American Catholics and Confession, 1900–1975," in *Habits of Devotion: Catholic Religious Practice in Twentieth-Century America*, ed. James M. O'Toole

there have been movements to reenergize this sacrament with a variety of approaches, it simply has not taken hold the way it dictated schedules in the 1940s, '50s, and '60s.

While the ultimate motivation for confession among most participants was fear of the worst and preparation for the best chance at heaven, another driving force was one's readiness to receive Holy Communion at Mass. Without a clear conscience and clean soul, one is considered unfit to participate in this sacrament in the Catholic tradition. Children must receive their first confession, then, before they can receive their first Holy Communion. As noted earlier, the pomp and circumstance surrounding this next event and the nuns' emphasis on precision communicated to students the importance of the sacrament. They recognized that this was, one way or another, a life-changing event. Donna Brazile (b. 1959), recalling her childhood as an African American in Louisiana, shows how for Catholics of the time, this was a before-and-after moment. Because of the importance of racial difference in her situation, however, her story offers a unique perspective on the weight of the sacraments. She remembers that upon the assassination of Bobby Kennedy, one of the Kennedys "who were famous in (their) household for being Catholic, too," her grandmother made the family go to a special Mass to mourn his death. She writes, "When we arrived, the Black folks had to sit in the back—as always. I did not like sitting in the back and I vowed when I completed my first holy communion and made my confirmation that I would sit up front like everyone else."[58] It was simple: life after these sacraments would be different. For Brazile, this meant that she would no longer be restricted in her church by the color of her skin.

---

(Ithaca, N.Y.: Cornell University Press, 2004). For an in-depth study of the changing notion of sin and the decline of the sacrament of penance since the mid-twentieth century, see Maria C. Morrow, *Sin in the Sixties: Catholics and Confession 1955–1975* (Washington, D.C.: The Catholic University of America Press, 2016).

58. Brazile, *Cooking with Grease*, 31.

For the Catholic children who did not have to face such preju-
dice in their parishes, there were other kinds of before-and-after
interpretations. Literary descriptions of the experience during
mid-century years reveal instances of theological confusion, stem-
ming from the solemn lessons and the schoolyard lore about just
what this experience would entail. As seven-year-olds were being
indoctrinated, their introductions to religious ritual were rarely tailored to young minds. The emphasis was placed not on any
thoughtful reflection about the sacrament's meaning, but rather
on an appreciation for its importance because it contained "the
real presence of Christ."

Such a mystifying concept at the center of this momentous rite
of passage finds its way into the literature. While many authors
focus on the complete misunderstanding experienced as communicants, others share a profound encounter with the depth of this
new act of faith. Anne Rice describes how her focus changed after
a poignant conversation about receiving the sacrament: "On the
day of my First Communion, the only thing I really cared about was
my white dress, my paper wreath of white flowers, and those I'd
visit afterwards as the special little girl who'd just made her First
Communion."[59] Attentive to the details in which one might expect
a child to relish, the feeling changes when she goes to Mercy Hospital to visit her aunt and the other nuns there. She writes, "I recall
an ancient nun, a kitchen sister, all in white with an apron, coming into the hospital garden and telling me with a radiant face that
this was a wonderful day because my soul was so pure . . . the look
of joy on her face and the enthusiasm with which she said these
words were breathtaking to me. She seemed utterly and completely
sincere in the present of a magnificent concept that went beyond
anyone or anything present." The white dress and wreath seem to

59. Rice, *Called Out of Darkness*, 63.

fade into the background after this conversation. Rice explains, "She is the memory of my First Communion, and I never knew her name."[60] It was important, holy, unmatched, and though the buildup may have focused on the surface, Rice shares the depth of the experience as it pertained to her soul.

Ron Hansen (b. 1947) depicts his own profound realization, as well, only he is able to come to it himself. He explains the preparation he, his twin brother, Rob, and their sixty classmates received before the special day: "We'd been catechized to feel awe for the mystery of Christ's presence in the sacrament we'd receive." He also shares the practical concerns leading up to this moment: "We'd heard from the older kids on the playground that the Host tasted terrible and Rob was afraid he'd hate it and yet be punished with hellfire if he spit it out." They had gathered that the details and one's response could have serious pragmatic consequence. For Ron, these deliberations on his First Communion drifted more to the changes he would experience: "Would I be a Superman, a holy man, a healer? Would homework now be easier? Would I be a wiz? Or would I be jailed in piety, condemned to sinlessness, obedience and no fun?"[61] The range of possibilities to the second-grader amusingly communicates the sense of wonder surrounding the experience. He did not know the direction his life would take, but he knew life would not be the same when he took in the Body of Christ. When he does finally receive the sacrament, he follows the protocol and does as he was instructed, but his mind starts to panic, "fancying Christ now sitting dismally in my scoundrel soul, my oh so many sins pooling like sewer water at his sandaled feet." Such a vivid image of his unworthy soul, however, does not last. Instead, the young boy comes to a new, indeed life-changing, realization:

60. Ibid., 64.
61. Ron Hansen, "Eucharist," in *Signatures of Grace*, 70.

"But soon I saw that I was still me; there would be no howls of objection, no immediate correction or condemnation, no hint that I was under new management, just the calming sense that whoever I was was fine with Jesus. It was a grace I hadn't imagined."[62] Prepared for the worst possibility and relieved by the best outcome, Hansen's story of his First Communion highlights the centrality of the soul in his young mind and the way its strong connection to the sacraments was instilled early. For Catholic children during the mid-twentieth century, the immortal soul was not a distant idea but an everyday concern. While few second-graders could probably claim such a poignant encounter with holiness, most would have shared in Hansen's curiosity and concern. With eternal life on the line, emerging Catholics internalized the potential impact of sin and sacraments.

While the Catholic faith has always contained tremendous mystery within its creed, the mid-twentieth-century institutional church in the United States provided a clear and direct way to practice its religion. The roles, rituals, and requirements were defined, respected, and rarely questioned. Children learned the faith so that they knew what they should be doing (or not) and what the potential consequences were of failing to meet those expectations. With the path to salvation so neatly marked, there remained little need for considering much else. It determined, overtly or not, most of a child's existence. This insular Catholic experience would transform during the 1960s and beyond. Even today, the church and the faith continue to emerge slowly from the Second Vatican Council and the decades that followed. But for those whose childhoods were characterized by that particular Catholic world, it was a formative, life-determining experience.

With the parish and its school at the center of formal religious ex-

---

62. Ibid., 71.

perience, cultural Catholicism of the 1940s, '50s, and '60s reached well beyond the church doors and into the home. In the next chapter, we shift away from this public domain into the intimate spaces of domestic life to see yet another context that has shaped a generation of Catholics.

# CHAPTER 3

# I Was Born
## a Catholic and I Think
## I Will Die One

∽≫∾

### Inheriting Religion in
### the Home

My post-college adventure teaching English in a small Mexican city had me feeling bold and brave as a young twenty-something in a foreign country, but it also left me feeling a long way from home. On my walk to campus, I passed a Catholic Church with pink walls and huge empty windows that minimized the separation between the sacred space and the surrounding sidewalk. For the first few weeks, I was too busy adjusting to a new job, a new place, and a new culture to go to Mass, but I occasionally felt a pull as I walked by. One day, I finally dragged myself to a pew. As I settled onto the kneeler and looked up to see the ever-familiar crucifix above the altar, I experienced a palpable connection to home and family, to my parents especially, who had probably already attended Mass that day in the parish where I was baptized and confirmed. Even though the Spanish language still sounded foreign and the open-air building was remarkably distinct from the stained glass that would have surrounded me back home, the rhythm and movement of the Mass united me to the people I was missing most. The universal church, I saw then, resonated for me because I had learned the importance of its faith and practices in the intimate space of home and in the context of family.

Catholicism certainly cannot claim a monopoly on being a religion shared and taught at home. This process is fairly standard for the survival of most religions. Still, among Catholics who narrate the experience of learning the faith at home in the mid-twentieth century, church membership was casually assumed and ultimately defining. For many, it seemed simply to run in the blood. "I am a Catholic by birth," writes Alice McDermott.[1] "I was born a Catholic and I think I will die one," explains Anna Quindlen.[2] Richard Rodriguez acknowledges, "I must confess—I am a Catholic by birth and by choice."[3] Born a Catholic. Catholic by birth. It felt like genetic inheritance. Fully aware that only the sacrament of baptism grants official entry into the Catholic Church, authors convey the presumed religious affiliation that came with family membership.

In this chapter, I examine the critical and complex role of the family within the cultural Catholicism of the mid-twentieth century. Here I move away from the desks and the kneelers to examine lessons within the home. Despite never having professed vows of ordination, parents and grandparents still had significant power for determining what it meant to be Catholic, and they offered the ever-important introduction before a child ever stepped foot in a classroom. Ed Stivender (b. 1946) remembers being ready for his first day of Catholic school. After significant preparation—receiv-

1. McDermott, "Confessions of a Reluctant Catholic," 12.
2. Quindlen, *Living Out Loud*, 159.
3. *Holy Visit, January 5, 1998*, PBS, 1998 (cited November 27, 2005); available from http://www.pbs.org/newshour/essays/january98/rodriguez_1–5.html.

ing school supplies, trying on his uniform, getting his hair cut—the six-year-old started Holy Cross Elementary. He knew he had been groomed in other important ways for this day: "My education as a Catholic had started long before now. . . . I had been going to Church with my mother since baptism and learned to recite the Hail Mary and most of the Our Father. I knew how to bless myself, genuflect and take off my hat in Church. I was primed for this moment."[4] Before any nun instructed him in the proper penitence for making confession or the required movements for receiving Holy Communion, this young Catholic had been schooled by his mother in the basics of prayer and practice.

When Anne Rice recalls how she learned about God, she writes, "What strikes me now as important about this experience is that it preceded reading books." Despite Christianity's characterization as a religion of the book, coming to understand the faith had little to do with literacy: "My concept of God came through the spoken words of my mother, and also the intensely beautiful experiences I had in church." As a small child, Rice was brought to a local chapel by her mother many evenings a week. She describes in vivid detail the walks to that place and the entire experience of their visits. Being introduced by her mother to the stories and images that surrounded her in the chapel, Rice came to know Jesus. She writes, "The concepts were not puzzling and they were part of life."[5]

Catholic life did not begin with enrollment in parochial school or even a first Mass. According to these authors, it began at birth. Their local Catholic world encompassed them immediately. For those members of the church born today to Catholic parents who plan to raise their children in the faith, that reality remains; religious experience begins at home. What has changed dramatically, though, is the surrounding context. During the decades of the

4. Ed Stivender, *Raised Catholic: Can You Tell?* (Little Rock: August House, 1992), 13–14.
5. Rice, *Called Out of Darkness*, 5, 6, 14.

1940s, '50s, and '60s, family life was mostly a private affair, perhaps extending into the neighborhood or to the parish through a rare consultation with a priest or prayerful consideration during a religious retreat. Families would be aware of things happening on the other side of the world, but mostly as a cause for prayerful intentions. They had a duty to offer spiritual appeals to heaven for those threatened by communism or hunger. Far-away places would not have offered a resource for integrating faith into family life. That has changed. In recent generations, many American Catholics have discovered a wide network of support for religious family life in the global Catholic community. For example, the World Meeting of Families brings together church members from all over the planet to consider the challenges and opportunities for religion in the home. Since its inception by Pope John Paul II in 1994, this triennial event has assembled church members in sites from Italy to the Philippines to Philadelphia, for consideration of and discussion about the sacred bonds of family. While Catholics in 1945 Philadelphia may have found themselves preparing for the local priest's visit, their descendants might have been readying their home to host a Catholic priest from Panama for the 2015 World Meeting of Families. Catholic girls of the 1950s expressed frustration at the private pressure to take vows, religious or marital; in 2015 a collection of international lay men and women professors addressed crowds on the role of marriage and the vitality of the Catholic family. While the local community remains just as much a focus for families today as in the 1940s, '50s, and '60s, families and local communities are no longer insulated from a pluralistic world as they might have felt decades ago.

Committed to the same church and raised in the same faith, Catholics today, like generations before them, recognize the primacy of the family at the heart of Christian life. With that truth at the center, the surrounding context has changed. Catholicism as birthright no longer seems sufficient for passing on the tradition. Living within this current American Catholic environment, writers who grew up decades ago represent a remarkably different experience of family and home life in their writing. The family home was simply one of the spaces in which Catholicism was part of one's reality and religious identity blended into the regular routines.

Stories from these mid-twentieth-century Catholic homes, then, bring readers into a world where family life was rarely a topic of discussion and instead an unspoken occasion for religious practice. While the narratives exhibit variety in the specific details, often as a result of the gender, ethnic, or personal differences among the writers, the literature indicates five aspects of family life that connect these authors to a Catholic heritage: (1) the practices that were observed and learned in the home, some of which became lifelong habits; (2) the objects and sacramentals that filled the spaces of the home and symbolized an atmosphere of piety and morality; (3) the validation of gendered roles and behavior based on ideal Catholic models; (4) the spoken and unspoken rules that governed sexual behavior; and (5) the association of one's identity as a son or daughter with one's identity as a Catholic. Through these representations, authors portray an inevitable religious identity that blended the institutional church's expectations with the everyday activity involved in family relationships and habits of the home.

### Prayer and Other Practices

My mother was the oldest of eight children. Her father, an attorney, served as the lawyer for their diocese. The church had an important presence in their home. Nobody close to them would be surprised to learn that they prayed together as a family. Still, my mother's sibling recalled to me the importance of remembering to take the phone off the hook during their daily rosary recitation. If no one remembered and the phone rang, they faced the choice of either letting it ring for what seemed like forever or answering it. The person who got stuck taking the call would have to tell the person at the other end that everyone was busy, with the din of nine others in the background, "Holy Mary, Mother of God. . . ." It was always a little awkward.

The middle decades of the twentieth century witnessed the impact of certain historical conditions, communism and secularism namely, which would influence the prayer life of American Catholic families. Historian Joseph Chinnici explains, "In general, the devotional life of the community looked in two directions: outward toward society and inward toward the family."[6] He describes the outward direction of devotion as combining loyalty to the church with loyalty to democracy in public ritual. Inwardly, he explains, "The family became a miniature Church, a small religious cloister, an enclave protected against secularism by its prayer and social order."[7] Two fundamental expressions of prayer life emerged: the campaign for the family rosary and the Enthronement of the Sacred Heart. The first meant the regular praying of the rosary, while the second involved the display and blessing of this religious image in the home.[8] With secularism and communism looming large somewhere far away, the family accepted the responsibility for doing what they could within their own homes to end it: pray. Even if that was not the motivating factor, families heeded the call to increase their devotion at home.

These religious rituals took a variety of forms. Mary Gordon recalls one of her family's rites that included the magic of television. In her autobiographical essay, "My Grandmother's House," she recalls regular visits for the special treat enjoyed by those Catholics

6. Joseph Chinnici, "The Catholic Community at Prayer, 1926–1976," in *Habits of Devotion*, 57.

7. Ibid., 59.

8. Ibid., 60.

who owned a television in the 1950s. She writes, "On Tuesdays, we went to her house to watch Bishop Sheen. Those nights after the moon vanished and the screen filled in its image, what you saw first was an empty chair. His. The bishop's. And then himself. . . ."[9] She describes the power his image carried even from a screen: "His eyes seemed transparent. They knew everything. They looked into your sinful soul."[10] The Catholic Church entered her family's space through this remarkable medium. They gathered and listened. It was time to be together with the bishop at the center. The show itself became the impetus for what followed: "After Bishop Sheen, we would go into the kitchen and kneel for the Rosary. Or my grandmother, my father and I would kneel. My mother and my aunt, both being crippled, were allowed to sit. After the regular prayers, we said a special prayer for the Conversion of Russia."[11] The church, with its message and its call, made its way regularly into their home, and Gordon's family responded through intimate, communal prayer, including one for the good of the world.

When television wasn't available, radio could also do the trick. Families might be found tuning their receivers to hear "The Rosary Priest," Fr. Patrick Peyton, whose regular program hosted celebrities for joint prayers to Mary over the airwaves. Fr. Peyton coined the phrase "The family that prays together stays together!" and made it his personal mission to bring families together to pray the rosary.[12] Radio brought religious practice directly into the home for Anne Rice, who recalls "the Rosary being recited every evening for fifteen minutes" and the regular broadcast of Sunday mass. She cites her grandmother's example of infusing this source for religious life into domestic life: "My grandmother, long unable to go to

9. Gordon, *Seeing through Places*, 31.

10. Ibid.

11. Ibid., 32.

12. "Father Patrick Peyton: Rosary Priest," *Father Patrick Peyton: Rosary Priest*, http://www.fatherpeyton.org/, accessed January 20, 2017.

church because of her broken hip and her built-up shoe, listened to the Mass in the dining room as she said her Rosary and read *Our Sunday Visitor*, a Catholic newspaper, all at the same time."[13] Nothing out of the ordinary, prayer and practice blended into regular routines.

Television and radio were not the only media that played major roles in family prayer. An even more common medium was the intercession of the saints. Claire Gaudiani (b. 1944) remembers, "The power of prayer infused everything we did as children. Prayer connected us to a world of heavenly expertise that we could draw on like senior partners or consultants. Saints and angels were there to help with all our needs, from lost mittens to lost causes: Saint Christopher when we traveled, Saint Francis when the cat was sick. . . ."[14] Nothing fell outside the realm of the saints and angels, and there seemed to be a specific name to call for any situation that could befall one. As she describes it, an awareness of this heavenly presence and the practice of calling upon these helpers had always been part of her world. This knowledge and the habits it prompted constitute much of what authors depict as the inheritance of their tradition.[15]

St. Anthony, patron saint of lost objects, has earned a confirmed spot in the memories of Catholic childhoods. Madeleine Blais suggests that his help was sought, perhaps, even a little too often: "Over the years, I have had the impression that we abused his goodwill, praying to him at the slightest hint of something's being missing,

13. Rice, *Called Out of Darkness*, 29–30.

14. Claire Gaudiani, "Of Cheese and Choices," in *Beyond the Godfather: Italian American Writers on the Real Italian American Experience*, ed. A. Kenneth Ciongoli and Jay Parini (Hanover, N.H.: University Press of New England, 1997), 118–19.

15. For more on this concept of religion outside institutional boundaries in U.S. religious history, see David D. Hall, *Lived Religion in America: Toward a History of Practice* (Princeton: Princeton University Press, 1997); Martin Marty, "Religion: A Private Affair, in Public Affairs," *Religion and American Culture* 3, no. 2 (1993); Orsi, *Madonna of 115th Street*.

even the most humble object, someone's misplaced hairbrush or pogo stick or Halloween candy."[16] I would guess that most Catholics born before 1980 could finish the prayer, "Dear St. Anthony, please come around. . . ."[17] During the middle of the twentieth century, the easy, automatic request for St. Anthony's assistance was becoming a habit that would remain with many for a lifetime.

Richard Rodriguez also recalls the regularity of prayer, particularly in times of need: "We prayed for favors and at desperate times. I prayed for help in finding a quarter I had lost on my way home. I prayed with my family at times of illness and when my father was temporarily out of a job. And when there was death in the family, we prayed."[18] Prayer could assist with every challenge in life, from the most mundane like lost quarters to the most momentous like a soul's salvation. It occurred always and everywhere. For Rodriguez, however, prayer was also a regular and ritualized event in the household. Once again, the rosary enters the scene: "Catholicism at home was shaped by the sounds of the 'family rosary': tired voices repeating the syllables of the Hail Mary; our fingers inching forward on beads toward the point of beginning; my knees aching; the coming of sleep."[19] Sometimes arduous, always embodied, the ritual was expected and enforced. Even though he complained about the posture and hour of this routine, prayer did offer the youngster comfort. He recalls, "Those nights when I'd shudder awake from a nightmare, I'd remember my grandmother's instruction to make a sign of the cross in the direction of my window. (That way Satan would find his way barred.) Sitting up in bed, I'd aim the sign of the cross against the dim rectangle of light. Quickly, then, I'd say the Prayer to My Guardian Angel, which would enable me to fall back

---

16. Blais, *Uphill Walkers*, 3.
17. ". . . something's lost and can't be found."
18. Rodriguez, *Hunger of Memory*, 85.
19. Ibid., 87.

asleep."[20] Whether in the middle of the day or the middle of the night, prayer had become a habitual activity. Observing and participating in both the unstructured and the synchronized moments of prayer, a young Rodriguez takes up the ritual as his own. It comes naturally and gives him peace.

Rodriguez's representation confirms that many Catholic practices, while encouraged by the church, are ultimately learned from and approved by the family. The feeling of security and support engendered by the ritual of prayer emerges directly from lessons by his parents and grandmother. Without that context, these practices would have little meaning for the youngster. Cultural Catholicism emerges when the overlapping worlds of church and family combine to produce inevitable religious norms.

A contrasting literary example provides a useful perspective for understanding this phenomenon. Esmeralda Santiago (b. 1948) does not experience an inevitable Catholic inheritance, despite witnessing the faith of her father and grandmother. In *When I Was Puerto Rican*, she describes how her father embraces a Catholic piety but her mother remains indifferent to religion, so Santiago finds herself confused and seeking answers. As evidenced in some of the preceding stories, grandmothers tend to exemplify prayerful devotion, and Santiago finds that to be true of her own. She expresses a longing for the elder's faithful practice. She remembers being at her grandmother's home: "From the stoop, I could hear the rhythmic clicks of her rosary beads and the soft hum of her voice reciting prayers whose music was familiar to me, but whose words I'd never learned. And I wished that I knew how to pray, because then I could speak to God and maybe He or one of His saints could explain things to me."[21] Unlike Gaudiani, Rodriguez, and Gordon, who had been drawn into their family's prayer life with little effort—at least

20. Ibid.
21. Esmeralda Santiago, *When I Was Puerto Rican* (New York: Vintage, 1994), 92–93.

as they interpret it—Santiago depicts a child yearning for meaning that others find in prayer. Its familiarity as a result of her father's and grandmother's regular practice makes it an appealing activity for her. The combination of rhythmic action, mystical belief, and a sense of belonging draw her to this religious ritual.

Santiago suspects and learns that there is a proper way of doing it. It requires the correct motions and words. We do it *this* way. After working her way slowly through the Our Father with her grandmother, stopping line by line to understand the meaning of each, she takes on the next task to discover the complicated nature of crossing herself. Her grandmother reviews each step, and the young girl reflects, "I'd seen women cross themselves so many times, it had never occurred to me that there was a right way and a wrong way to do it."[22] This was a crucial gesture to master, because her grandmother had explained that it was a mandatory part of saying the Lord's Prayer. After much rehearsal by Santiago, she is finally ready and works to perfect not only the words and gestures, but also the overall embodied reverence that she has carefully observed.

Catholic practice requires knowing what to do and how to do it, and that can only be learned by children when someone teaches it. So while it may have been felt, by some, that Catholic devotion was simply an inherited trait, Santiago's example reminds readers that family elders were constantly modeling and sharing their religious habits. Such lessons had a way of fading into the background.

### Artifacts and Images

Finding just the right-sized box to set up my May altar to Mary in my bedroom during my elementary school years always proved a challenge. A covered shoe box would not allow enough space for

22. Ibid., 101.

my items. A table took up too much room and seemed less intimate than something I could kneel before. Most years, I settled for the same cinderblock square covered by a piece of cardboard and a borrowed table linen from my mother. I hunted for all the Mary prayer cards, plastic rosaries, and artificial flowers I could find to make a proper altar suitable for the May Queen. It usually lasted well into the summer when the items eventually got scattered until the next year's ritual assembly. I don't recall any of my three siblings dedicating bedroom space to May altars; still, I looked forward to it every year. Unless I revive this tradition from my youth, it's hard to imagine that my elementary school–aged daughter might ever be inspired to construct one of her own. While the nuns at my school regularly encouraged this home practice, it is unlikely that anyone in my daughter's world would even know what it is.

The cultural Catholicism of the mid-twentieth century, whose influence I experienced even a few decades later, included not only prayerful practice but also physical reminders of the religious tradition. Statues, relics, portraits, and other religious objects filled the spaces of children's intimate worlds and filled their minds with meaning. Religious objects and articles occupied many different spaces for Catholic families: bedrooms, parlors, and even car dashboards. Maria Laurino (b. 1959) recalls her grandmother's bedroom: "Her dresser was her private place of worship, her altar. On it, votive candles flickered in ruby red glass, and statues of Mary, Saint Joseph, and Saint Anthony cast a quiet calm alongside several crucifixes."[23] Gina Cascone recalls the safety she felt riding in her grandmother's car: "We traveled in the company of Jesus, Mary and Christopher. Jesus and Mary stood in two circular dents in the dashboard. All the cars I'd seen had these two indentations—min-

---

23. Maria Laurino, *Were You Always an Italian?: Ancestors and Other Icons of Italian America* (New York: W. W. Norton, 2000), 158.

imum safety standards, two saints."[24] She notes that her grandmother even had the added feature of an *extra* saint in Christopher. Madeleine Blais describes her own bedroom: "Tucked behind the crucifix above the radiator were the dried-out palms we had gotten at church on the last Palm Sunday, and during one especially pious interval we even had a vessel with holy water for blessing ourselves every time we entered or exited our room."[25] Adults and children alike effortlessly interacted with the *stuff* of their faith.

As a black Catholic in New Orleans, Donna Brazile's experience was not the same as most of the authors in this study. Investigating the consequence of racial difference on religion at home would likely require another book entirely. Still, the prominence of religious objects would have easily linked her to her white coreligionists. She writes, "Being a good Catholic, my father had his altar right outside his *bouvetroire*, in a little alcove. There was the altar and there were two tiers so you could kneel and pray before it. It was a little scary, but no one dared drink or curse in front of the altar." More than just a means to ward off bad behavior, the altar and other religious objects had a more important function. Speaking of her father, Brazile explains, "He had all sorts of statues of St. Anthony, the Blessed Mother Mary, St. Michael and several crucifixes all throughout the house. With twelve mouths to feed, Lionel Brazile needed all the prayers he could get. Prayer was a daily act for all of us. It was mandatory."[26] Statues and crucifixes inspired habitual devotion.

Images of Jesus, particularly the Sacred Heart, feature prominently in stories about growing up Catholic. Mary Gordon and Richard Rodriguez offer rich descriptions of distinct reactions to these icons. Being surrounded by such items had various effects on

24. Cascone, *Pagan Babies*, 97.
25. Blais, *Uphill Walkers*, 97.
26. Brazile, *Cooking with Grease*, 8.

young children: at times, it yielded a sense of company and protection; at others, it produced fear. Mary Gordon recalls religious images in her grandmother's bedroom: "A picture of Christ with long, smooth, girlish hair, pointing to his Sacred Heart, the size and shape of a pimento or a tongue. Most mysterious: a picture made of slat. You turned your head one way: it was the scourging at the pillar. Another turn of the head produced Jesus Crowned with Thorns. If you looked absolutely straight ahead, you saw the Agony in the Garden. I spent hours looking at that picture, frightened, uncomprehending."[27] This mystifying picture, with its multiple images, overwhelms the young Gordon, and, still, she reports she could not resist looking at it.

On the other hand, Richard Rodriguez describes a picture of the Sacred Heart, given to his family by a priest, that he barely notices. It hung in a prominent position in the front room of every house in which his parents ever lived: "It has been one of the few permanent fixtures in the environment of my life. Visitors to our house doubtlessly noticed it when they entered the door—saw it immediately as the sign we were Catholic. But I saw the picture too often to pay it much heed."[28] The ever-present indication of his family's religion had become an unremarkable part of his home.[29]

Monica Wood shares a similar story of defining objects. When her family eventually had to move to a place that would accommodate her mother's new wheelchair, she notes the objects that had filled their original home within an apartment building owned by the Norkus family. As they carry them down the three flights of stairs, the items' poignancy resonates: "The jewelry box. The turkey pan. The kitchen chairs and the birdcage. The adding machine.

27. Gordon, *Seeing through Places*, 25.
28. Rodriguez, *Hunger of Memory*, 82.
29. For more on the role of religious imagery, see David Morgan, *Visual Piety: A History and Theory of Popular Religious Images* (Berkeley: University of California Press, 1998).

The toy piano. The pictures of Pope John and President John and the Sacred Heart of Jesus. The things we carried had made the Norkus block our home, the only one we'd ever known."[30] Religious artifacts travel right alongside the turkey pan and toys.

Not only did these images surround Monica Wood during her childhood, she describes the instinct to create them as a young girl. She remembers the days when her dad, who worked at the paper mill, brought home a ream, "a thing of creaseless beauty." Wood narrates the first thing they did with it: "Cathy and I drew pictures: nuns and angels; God the Father; God the Son; God the Holy Ghost with his flappy, histrionic wings."[31] There were other characters and places to depict, but they usually started with these. Powerful and holy, these images were part of the children's familiar world, easily lending themselves to her artistic interpretation, despite their religious importance.

Whether producing a feeling of security or terror or sometimes simply fading into the scenery, these articles and images contribute to religious identities that were formed during youth and persist into adulthood.[32] In a similar vein to Rodriguez, Rita Ciresi demonstrates how familial Catholic objects blend into her surroundings even in her adult life. Her fiction offers rich examples of this continuous engagement with Catholic images and objects. The narrator in her story "The Little Ice Age" notes, "I . . . was guilty of habit, of keeping things in the same old place. Even though I hadn't lived in my parents' house for years, I still carried the key with me every day. It was attached to a silver key tag that depicted the Vatican." She lists the random assortment of things at the bottom of her purse, which includes "a St. Christopher holy card that said

30. Wood, *When We Were the Kennedys*, 228.
31. Ibid., 98.
32. For a study of the function of material culture in the religious lives of Americans, see McDannell, *Material Christianity: Religion and Popular Culture in America* (New Haven, Conn.: Yale University Press, 1995).

on the back CATHOLIC: In case of accident, call a priest."[33] Given to her by her mother, these two items rolling around in her pocketbook link her to her family and their Catholicism. Ciresi's protagonist in the novel *Pink Slip* describes walking through a museum with her Jewish boyfriend, Strauss. They enter a room filled with plates depicting religious scenes. She reports, "I felt Catholicism emanating from every pore in my body. I wondered how Strauss reacted to these repeated images of the Annunciation, the Adoration of the Magi, the Madonna and Child, the Crucifixion, the Deposition. What was it like not to believe in Christ in a world full of crosses?"[34] The pictures and crucifixes trigger religious reflection. A powerful feature from her past, they tie her to a Catholic perspective and make it difficult to imagine growing up with anything different.

Each of the examples noted so far connects the interactions with Catholic material culture to the family members who offered instruction about these items. Without the mothers', grandmothers', and aunts' association with these religious objects, they would not possess the same meaning. This material culture and its special connection to family members affect the religious identities of those who occupied this cultural Catholicism.

### Assumed and Assigned Gender Roles

My maternal grandmother was Mary. My mother was Maryanne, and I am Mary Ellen. (My dad, by the way, is Joseph.) It's hard to deny my Catholic roots—they are spelled out right in the name. Perhaps that is why I felt called to erect a May altar each year. It was an annual opportunity to acknowledge my patron saint. Oddly enough, I never felt that the Virgin Mother received dispropor-

33. Rita Ciresi, "The Little Ice Age," in *Sometimes I Dream in Italian* (New York: Dell, 2000), 132.

34. Ciresi, *Pink Slip*, 188.

tionate attention in my home as we grew up. She was a major part of the story, of course, but her role remained part of that long-ago narrative and rarely an example for contemporary life. I don't know that my mother could say the same—there was daily rosary in her household, after all. Certainly the writers of her generation also paint a different picture of an imitable model in that ever Virgin mother.

The gendered dynamics of religious devotion at home surface regularly in the tales of mid-twentieth-century Catholic life. In the next chapter, I will look specifically at ethnic influences upon such dynamics, but here I consider perceived roles of women and men. To be sure, countless authors recall the days when mothers and grandmothers dragged them to Mass, but rather than observe gendered liturgical participation, my goal in this section is to identify the lessons learned at home about domestic religious responsibilities and, incidentally, the making of a good Catholic woman.

Recalling the playful banter about saints and commandments enjoyed among her uncles, Maria Laurino writes, "These men played with faith, letting the women, the madonnas, be the standard-bearers of devotion, but never abandoned their religion. Men could be scoundrels like Saint Aloysius and of course be forgiven for their sins—as long as the women did the praying for them."[35] As the standard-bearers of devotion, women are depicted here as maintaining significant responsibility for religion in the home and for the souls of their loved ones. Their piety demanded a commitment to the moral standards expected of a Catholic woman during these middle decades of the twentieth century. Among the most crucial of these were chastity and motherhood. Patricia Hampl writes, "The purpose of a Catholic education for girls was to produce good Catholic wives and mothers. No bones about that pre-feminist intention. The mod-

35. Laurino, *Were You Always an Italian?*, 158.

el was—who else?—Mary, the Virgin Mother."[36] As a result of statues and prayer cards and fervent devotion, the Virgin Mary became a common household name. She provided the model example for womanhood. Historian Paula Kane writes, "The 1950s consolidated the conservative ideals of Catholic womanhood that had been on the rise throughout the century. . . . At a religious level, a rhetoric of purity chose to emphasize the Madonna's motherhood, home-making and modesty, and was especially addressed to adolescent girls."[37] The most esteemed role for a woman was chaste wife and devoted mother. Both Kane and Hampl note the ultimate example provided: the ever-virgin Mary, Mother of God. The home, then, became a critical context for the display of women's true religious devotion. What they did and did not do in the bedroom mattered. How they provided for their husbands and children in the kitchen and living rooms largely determined their virtue.

The weight of proper parenting also fell largely to women, according to depictions in this literature. In her novel *Men and Angels*, Mary Gordon's character Anne, an art historian, and her friend Barbara consider the biases of history when evaluating the artists of the past. In a conversation about the subject of Anne's research, artist Caroline Watson, the two discuss the unfair criteria for judging talent. Anne says, "Sometimes I want to slam her for being a bad mother, then sometimes I think it didn't matter, she was a great painter, so what was the difference." Barbara replies, "Nobody gives a shit if Monet was a bad father."[38] Gordon's fictional characters give voice to the frustration experienced in some Catholic households because of a double standard applied to women.

Catholic households were not the only ones dealing with this expectation during the middle decades of twentieth-century Amer-

36. Hampl, *Virgin Time*, 62.
37. Kane, "Marian Devotion since 1940," 104.
38. Mary Gordon, *Men and Angels*, large print ed. (Boston: G. K. Hall, 1986), 171.

ica. Betty Friedan's 1963 publication *The Feminine Mystique* drew attention to the construction of femininity among the entire middle class in the United States. In this segment of society, she argued, women became prisoners in their own homes. Authors narrating a mid-twentieth-century cultural Catholicism belong to the generation that responded to Friedan's critique and have witnessed how such responses ultimately led to the reform labeled "second-wave feminism." A complicated movement, one of its results included new socially acceptable definitions of true womanhood. Such a massive cultural shift certainly influences these authors' reflections on their childhood homes. With broader conceptions of women than what would have been available to them then, many authors express frustration about the circumstances that typified their youth.[39]

Still, firmly situated in the social milieu of their times, writers emphasize that the gendered norms they learned were often, even within this broad historical context, specific to their religious tradition. The focus on the Virgin Mary, for example, communicates a choice to highlight the Catholic nature of their situations. Martha Manning has remarked about Mary, "Through her I received the Catholic church's formulation of the perfect woman. I had it hammered into me, year after year, that Mary was the model to which I should aspire: pure, passive, and docile."[40] When Anna Quindlen

---

39. "Gender" as a historical category has only developed in recent decades; see Joan W. Scott, "Gender: A Useful Category of Historical Analysis," *American Historical Review* 91, no. 5 (1986). For a historical survey of gender in the United States, see Sylvia D. Hoffert, *A History of Gender in America: Essays, Documents, and Articles* (Upper Saddle River, N.J.: Prentice Hall, 2003). For considerations of feminism and reform movements, see Daniel Horowitz, *Betty Friedan and the Making of the Feminine Mystique: The American Left, the Cold War, and Modern Feminism* (Amherst: University of Massachusetts Press, 1998); Blanche Linden-Ward and Carol Hurd Green, *American Women in the 1960s: Changing the Future* (New York: Twayne, 1993); Winifred D. Wandersee, *On the Move: American Women in the 1970s* (Boston: Twayne, 1988). For considerations of gender as it relates to race and ethnicity, see Karen Anderson, *Changing Woman: A History of Racial Ethnic Women in Modern America* (New York: Oxford University Press, 1996); Deborah G. White, *Too Heavy a Load: Black Women in Defense of Themselves, 1894–1994* (New York: W. W. Norton, 1999).

40. Manning, *Chasing Grace*, 141.

reflects on her limited options as a female, she writes, "Part of my dissatisfaction with my life was clearly, in retrospect, a dissatisfaction with the traditional roles available to me as a girl at the time, neither of which—nun or housewife, take your pick—particularly suited my temperament."[41] Quindlen depicts her perceived choices as closely tied to her Catholicism. Her readers can imagine her childhood environment as one where life in the convent would be an admirable pursuit. So, daily existence for women, in these literary representations, involved specific obligations to Catholic expectations. In behavior and manner, girls were to emulate the Virgin Mary. With regard to lifelong interests, motherhood and sisterhood (in the formal sense, of course) offered the most venerable options.

Even the cinema of the 1940s lauded the Blessed Mother's example and the commensurate suffering that seemed to accompany the purest kind of devotion for females. *The Song of Bernadette* (1943) depicted the miracle story of Mary's apparition to a young, ailing child in the town of Lourdes, France, in 1848. After struggling to convince anyone of her visions, young Bernadette can finally offer proof when, at Mary's request, the girl digs in the dirt to reveal a miraculous spring that issues healing waters. As onlookers try to make sense of this healing water, she continues to face doubt and ridicule. Eventually, she is led to believe that the convent is the best, and only, option for her, even though she might prefer an ordinary life. Within religious life, she faces terrible hardship under strict supervisors. Ultimately, though, when it is discovered she has been enduring a painful form of tuberculosis, she is admired for suffering with grace and dies surrounded by her fellow sisters in prayer. Members of the film's 1940s audience would have likely known someone who possessed a small bottle of this healing water from Lourdes in real life.

41. Anna Quindlen, *How Reading Changed My Life*, Library of Contemporary Thought (New York: Ballantine, 1998), 27.

Their familiarity with this Marian miracle tale combined with the film's portrayal of Bernadette's ever-suffering holiness on the big screen made Catholic gender expectations a ubiquitous force.

Author Catherine Gildiner's mother offers a curious alternative, though, to this typical perspective of the ever-sacrificing woman and mother. Gildiner recalls playing at her friend's house and witnessing her friend's mom "always taking care of a baby or cooking or ironing." When the girl mentions this observation to her own mother and wonders why someone would have to do all that work, Gildiner's mom admits to wondering the same, particularly why anyone would have more than one baby. "She thought the odd part," continues Gildiner, "was that women considered themselves holy or virtuous when they had houses bursting with six children. My mother reminded me that the Holy Family had only one child, as our family did." Her mother also advised young Catherine to never learn to cook or type for fear of the consequence: "You'd be requested to do both against your will forever." When the girl describes her friend's mom's ironing habits—she "even ironed *bed* linen"—her mother replies that "Mrs. Canavan would someday be a saint." She went on to advise her daughter, though, to throw away any irons she might someday receive as wedding gifts "because there might be too much of a temptation to use them."[42] Gildiner's mother clearly contradicts the typical Catholic view of a woman's role at home, but still, even as she passes this on to her daughter she invokes Catholic concepts. Bucking the trend, this woman emphasizes an unconventional way of emulating the Holy Family, particularly the Virgin Mother, with her singular child. Still, readers are left to wonder if her sainthood comment pokes fun at the typical perception or confirms a respect for martyrdom. The young Gildiner would not have suspected sarcasm, and so the scene provides one more example of the culturally

42. Gildiner, *Too Close to the Falls*, 63–64.

Catholic world that enveloped children, even if it was not the most conventional.

For many, the woman's place in the home issued a direct challenge and yielded frustration because of perceived limitations. Other writers, however, exhibit ambivalence about this point. In fact, some writers recognize the strength of their mothers because of their very place in the home. Claire Gaudiani exemplifies such a response: "Although our mother never worked outside the home, my brothers and sisters and I always felt she had great power through the simplicity of prayer.... Our mother's prayer life, anchored in her parents' faith, created an awesome example of a powerful woman as I looked back on my childhood."[43] Rather than denying a woman a role in public, Catholicism in this representation gives a woman power at home. Gaudiani does not portray her mother as a disenfranchised person, but rather one who gladly accepts her role in the family and fulfills it with strength and achievement.

With such a multitude of examples in which girls may have experienced certain pressures, one might wonder whether boys, too, felt expectations as a result of Catholic mothers' piety. John Bernard Ruane describes his situation: "My mother, Therese McInerney Ruane, was like a number of devout Irish-American Catholic mothers and wanted one of her sons to become a priest.... Because of my love for her and the desire to make her proud of me, I began the path to ordination that began with becoming an altar boy."[44] Ruane does not pursue the path much beyond this first step, but the memory of his motivation does communicate a gendered, albeit ethnically understood, norm at home.

In another ethnically charged perception, one man, who actually did pursue the path to its conclusion, remembers a different kind of expectation. Bishop Francis G. Mugavero (1914–91) grew

43. Gaudiani, "Of Cheese and Choices," 119.
44. Ruane, *Parish the Thought*, 47.

up a little earlier than most of my subjects discussed so far, but his recollection of a gendered model reveals a strong culture of norms. When asked what high school he wanted to attend in Brooklyn, New York, the teenager answered "Cathedral." This was the place for boys who wanted to become priests. He describes his mother and father's reaction: "Both parents hoped I would change my mind about Cathedral. Their thinking was, What is this becoming a priest and leading a celibate life? Full-blooded, normal Italian boys find a girl, get married, and raise a family."[45] He did not change his mind and went on to become the bishop of Brooklyn. This decision did not harm his relationship with his parents. In fact, the bishop says about his own family and others, "I think the greatest contribution Italian-Americans have made to our culture is the example of the caring, close-knit family—of a family that is *concerned* and knows how to make sacrifices for one another."[46] The next chapter pursues these emphases on ethnic influences; through these examples, readers witness males whose Catholic parents convey clear expectations about gendered roles.

When it comes to experienced religion at home, mothers and grandmothers do tend to receive the most attention in stories of Catholic childhood, even by male writers. As noted, the focus on the Virgin Mary probably skews things in that direction. Acknowledging this disparity, we are left with a question: where are the men, the fathers, in these settings? They do receive mentions from time to time. In many ways, they were the rule keepers who made certain the family stayed in line with demands from outside the home. Alice McDermott recalls her dad's regular contribution to the family's religion: "My father, in the great tradition of Catholic fathers everywhere, proclaimed, 'As long as you're living in my house you'll go to Mass on Sunday,' and then added, always, in a

45. Bishop Francis J. Mugavero, "Italian among the Irish," in *Growing Up Italian*, 101.
46. Ibid., 105.

softer, wearier tone, 'Trust me. You'll need the church as you get older. You don't think you need it now, but as you live, you'll see. Trust me.'"[47] He was not instituting family prayer, but rather insisting on his children's participation in the church. In this passage, McDermott clearly illustrates the in-charge attitude her father assumed with regard to his children's religion.

In Anna Quindlen's novel *Object Lessons*, the patriarch of the family, John Scanlan, insists that his granddaughter memorize the lists and information that he deems indicative of a good Catholic. Quindlen writes, "Maggie had been able to recite the deadly sins since first grade. The apostles were a throwaway question. Most recently her grandfather had asked her to recite from memory the Passion According to St. Mark, and Maggie had been amazed when she learned it successfully."[48] Resembling the exercises in the Catholic classroom, Scanlan drills young Maggie on her memorization of key Catholic data. This repetition, he assures her, will keep her firmly connected to the one true faith.

With women exemplifying piety and virtue and men upholding the rules and tradition, the family dynamics of mid-twentieth-century cultural Catholicism take shape in these narratives about growing up. Although certain themes emerge, Catholic families undoubtedly had their own idiosyncrasies that supplied limitless variations on gendered expectations. Still, this selection of memories offers a window into that experience of an all-encompassing religious world. As the nuns and priests were educating students in the conventions of the church, parents and grandparents were training children to participate in domestic Catholicism and issuing norms for their participation in the faith.

47. Alice McDermott, "Confessions of a Reluctant Catholic," 12.
48. Anna Quindlen, *Object Lessons* (New York: Fawcett Books, 1991), 38.

## Laws and Limits on Sex

The gendered roles and relationships that govern these narrated Catholic households affected not only one's perceived path in life or inferred household duties, but also had enormous ramifications for what one could do with his or her body, particularly in the bedroom. Sexuality, and its implied sinfulness in much of this literature, introduced another host of issues for children to navigate. For Patricia Hampl, a lesson about acceptable sexual behavior in one's personal life emerges powerfully from the public lessons about the saints. She narrates a discovery about the models of the church whose lives were to be emulated: "Most of the women saints in the Missal had under their names the designation *Virgin and Martyr*, as if the categories were somehow a matched set. Occasionally a great female canonized for her piety and charitable works received the label *Queen and Widow*. The men were usually *Confessor*, or, sometimes *Martyr*, but none of them was ever *Virgin*."[49] Hampl's narration stresses that the very holiness of women in the canon of saints demanded a certain sexual status: either virgin or widow. Certainly, men were equally called upon to live chastely; however, Hampl's observation suggests that men's sexual status did not receive the same notice as women's. This discreet message laid a certain groundwork for girls who could only grasp its implications later in life.

In her essay "Immaculate Heart," Susan Cokal (b. 1965) shares how conflicting attention to her sexuality during elementary school in Lynchburg, Virginia, and a discovery about her own mother's history have lasting effects into adulthood. She describes a playground pastime that has consequences: "We are playing our favorite game. We play it every day. We play it under the spreading oak tree, behind the red library that used to be a barn, west of the

49. Hampl, *Virgin Time*, 48–49.

white statue of the Virgin where the other girls lay roses and lilies and sticks of chewing gum." Inevitably the nuns will approach to break it up. "I am a bad girl, they tell me," she writes, "a dirty little girl." She details the game: "I am its goal. The boys rush at me and I stand still, push them hard to the ground if I like them, harder still if I don't; after two or three pushes, perhaps, I let one special boy come close, let his special lips graze my cheek, my brow, my lips."[50] Her teachers, the nuns, strongly condemn this behavior and do what they can to stop it: "Eventually mother is called and told of the dirty thing her daughter is doing. My mother, who will die when I am twenty-eight and still unmarried, giggles riotously and ruffles my hair, telling me she always played with the boys when she was little." Her mother's response was supportive, but it causes confusion when Cokal later learns about her mother's past. She writes, "I will learn that when my mother was in college in the 1960s she had a scholarship but it was taken away because she was dating a black boy. And that she married because she was pregnant with me. And I might just possibly not be the child of the man I call Daddy. I will be terrified by this information, from the top of my uncombed head to the scuffy toes of my too-tight saddle shoes."[51] The rules governing whom one could date, what they could do, and how to maintain a certain image land heavily upon this young girl's reality. They affect her deeply, and yet they remain confusing and scary.

Confusion likewise governs her efforts to navigate adolescence. She remembers, "(The nuns) tell me no girl my age has come to any good playing with boys. They don't tell me why this is dangerous and bad, only that it is. They don't tell me how the rushing game is different from sitting with Stephen, working on Thinklab cards

---

50. Susan Cokal, "Immaculate Heart," in *Resurrecting Grace: Remembering Catholic Childhoods*, ed. Marilyn Sewell (Boston: Beacon, 2001), 142.
51. Ibid., 143–44.

and listening to fish stories; they just say that it is."[52] There are clear expectations and assumptions, with little explanation or understanding. This unsettling combination of external voices leads to a profound internal disquiet within Cokal. Years later, having returned to the site of these games with her husband, she reflects on how the Virgin's imposed example looms large: "My husband will already know that I was actually a virgin until twenty-two, that I didn't even enjoy sex until my thirties, that mine was a long lonely adolescence as the kids at Immaculate Heart joined the nuns in thinking I was somehow unclean. Then we will walk to the oak tree and I will put my arms around him and we will come together in one long, willing kiss in the presence of sin, even as the Immaculate Heart still beats, heavy, inside me."[53] The Virgin, the nuns, and a mother's story yield a painful journey toward sexual maturity for this young girl.

Patricia Hampl reveals another way Catholic sexual mores could have consequence for girls raised with them. They might seem harmless, but they created assumptions that felt stultifying. And yet, the very experience of growing up in the environment made it difficult to reject such assumptions. She recalls a maddening moment as an adult, "'You're so ... wholesome,' a man at a cocktail party said when I was past forty. 'I hope you don't mind my saying so.' I minded. I seethed, but I was crushed by my old convent courtesy and smiled the smile." She notes the invariable response she has received when in diverse settings, both social and professional, she has commented that she "*should* do this or that": "the smooth voice of someone I hardly know, speaking from the authority of a secular background told me, 'Ah, that's your Catholic good-girl background again.'" The accumulation of such interactions builds to the point of rejecting that label. She explains, "I wanted to betray

52. Ibid., 144–45.
53. Ibid., 146–47.

it all, wanted to join that real world where no good girls are allowed, except as decorative touches here and there." The reason for such rejection, though, was not merely a concern over others' opinions, but rather something much deeper in her own self-perception: "I was terrified I was missing out on Life, that thing called 'experience,' all because I had been held in the cooing Catholic embrace too long and was forever marked. But marked by what? The indelible brand of innocence, which is to be marked by an absence, a vacancy, by nothing at all."[54] The praise for self-sacrifice and the connection between virginity and goodness came at a cost.

In her memoir, *Don't Get Me Started*, comic Kate Clinton (b. 1947) details the imparted lessons on sexual ethics from her religion and religious household: "According to my mother and to Mother Church, the only purpose of sex was to be a mother, and since I knew I was not going to be having kids, I resigned myself to the fact there would be no sex for me." While the reality was serious, she brings humor to its depiction: "The antisex force field of my youth— God, the guardian angel Snitch with the Tripp wire on my right, my mother, her spies, the church—was like a sex surveillance system with hidden cameras and heat sensitive sprinklers." The message was clear: no sex. Or you would be found out. And no one wanted to know what happened after that. She remembers the first time her mother spoke to her about sex in what she describes as an "erotocryptic" way: "Sex is dirty; save it for someone you love."[55] The odd combination of disdain and respect for sex made it seem important but harmful. Things got even more complicated for Clinton when she realized that she was a lesbian. She writes about her first sexual encounter "in a Dodge Colt in Boston's Back Bay after a St. Patrick's Day Parade." It went well, according to her amusing description, but then, "Unfortunately we were both Irish Catholic, first-born girls

54. Hampl, *Virgin Time*, 207.
55. Kate Clinton, *Don't Get Me Started* (New York: Ballantine, 1998), 88.

and what became a relationship crumbled under the weight of guilt and shame." Her story does not end sadly, though. Again, she wittily describes a quick recovery: "Thankfully, my next relationship was with a woman who had been raised Quaker and had no concept of guilt. Try as I might."[56] Clinton uses humor to depict the grim implications of the culture around sex and the prohibition against homosexuality that characterized her youth.

Such lightness around this grave topic, however, does not fairly address the painful reality for homosexuals raised in these religious milieus. Often with little understanding about their own sexual identities, they were regularly hearing about the evils and psychological ills of same-sex attraction. Philip Gambone (b. 1948) grew up near Boston with what he calls an "obligatory, letter-of-the-law Catholicism." In his essay "Searching for Real Words" in the collection *Wrestling with the Angel: Faith and Religion in the Lives of Gay Men*, he narrates his relationship to this clear-cut Catholicism: "As a boy, I went along with it unquestioningly."[57] He describes an important comfort about this religious certainty: "It removed most—if not all—of the ambiguity about who one was and how one needed to behave in this world. I grew up with the clear understanding that God wanted me to be a 'good boy' which pretty much meant that I should not transgress His laws and the laws of His Holy Catholic Church."[58] Obeying these laws did not create many problems until puberty. Until then the lessons about virgin martyrs and the crucial difference between love and lust had little impact. During adolescence, the message became clear, though: "Erotic pleasure of any kind violated the true purpose of the body, which was to be a 'temple of Christ.'"[59]

So with the onset of sexual longing, temptation and sin became

56. Ibid., 89.
57. Philip Gambone, "Searching for Real Words," in *Wrestling with the Angel: Faith and Religion in the Lives of Gay Men*, ed. Brian Bouldrey (New York: Riverhead, 1995), 222.
58. Ibid.
59. Ibid., 223.

real problems. He dutifully confessed his "impure thoughts and actions" each week, but it got more complicated when he found a buddy from his confirmation class to accompany him in these behaviors. He writes, "Every Tuesday, after we had sat through another lesson about the sacrament the bishop would confer upon us that spring, we'd go to my house or his and 'mess around.'" What became clear was that these mutual masturbation sessions meant different things to each boy. For his friend, it was just something to do. For Gambone, though, it had much greater meaning: "Although I didn't have words to describe what I was feeling, for me there was a dimension to our weekly clandestine get-togethers that went beyond the casual. In some unverbalized way, I understood that erotically touching another boy—being with a boy that way—was going to be a fundamental, inescapable aspect of who I was."[60] When his friend decides they have gotten "too old" for this activity, Gambone tries to convince him otherwise. The boy's refusal to continue becomes a kind of condemnation for the young Gambone: "I heard panic in his voice—maybe even some disgust. The fact that he was an altar boy (and I wasn't) made it worse: Clearly he was a better Catholic than I, one who had mustered the moral fortitude to turn away from such sins."[61] Over the next few years, Gambone tried to immerse himself in other activities that might distract him from those "feelings that had no name and no foreseeable outlet." Still, he was not able to completely shut down his "impure thoughts and actions." So he continued to confess and was assured by his confessor, "It's the seed, wanting to come out, the seed that God has planted in you, whose proper use is for the procreation of children with your wife after marriage."[62] And that was that: sex was only for married couples—a man and woman—so that they might reproduce.

60. Ibid.
61. Ibid., 224.
62. Ibid.

Throughout his early adulthood, Gambone struggled with his competing self-identities as a homosexual and a Roman Catholic. He found solace in the Episcopal faith of a man who became his first love because that religious world provided him "divine permission." "It was the only way," he explains, "I could come to accept my homosexuality."[63] Later in life, he finds himself moving back toward Roman Catholicism, the religion that feels most authentic, even as he struggles, as a gay man, to determine his relationship to it and place within it. Such effort to remain connected to a church that condemns him for acting on his love for another man raises important questions about the nature and depth of a Catholic identity. The formative experiences of his youth make it nearly impossible for him to abandon it altogether. That aspect of his identity rivals in importance his sexual orientation so that he accepts the complicated challenge of pursuing a full life as a gay Catholic man.

Another sexual issue that has found Catholics struggling against the imposed expectations of the church, particularly as exemplified during the mid-twentieth century, is the issue of reproductive rights. The debate over abortion emerges in these writings, but a subtler, and perhaps more pervasive, question is the challenge of contraception.[64] Paul Baumann (b. 1951) offers a male perspective on the example of his mother, who set the tone for his household. Even though he himself would never have to decide whether to take the Pill, his witness to his mother's experience and the message it conveyed shares a powerful story of life in these Catholic households. Baumann explains that his mother had a "firmly fixed view of the moral universe." It could easily be summarized: "No premarital sex, no extramarital sex, and no divorce were the fundamental

63. Ibid., 232.
64. For a detailed study of this issue in American Catholic history, see Leslie Woodcock Tentler, *Catholics and Contraception: An American History* (Ithaca, N.Y.: Cornell University Press, 2004).

articles of her faith, and on two or three occasions she explicated with startling crudeness the moral reasoning behind these prohibitions. (As I recall, it had something to do with cows and free milk.)"[65] These rules applied to men as much as to women, but women faced another set of conditions. He writes, "For women of her generation, 'a bad reputation' could put you on the marital sidelines, and out-of-wedlock pregnancy spelled exile or worse." A shared common knowledge meant that everyone knew the risk and consequences of unchaste sexual behavior, especially for females.

Still, even for those in chaste marriages, the church's prohibition against birth control created serious dilemmas for faithful Catholics. Baumann notes that, after seven pregnancies (two miscarriages and five healthy births), his mother suffered serious health complications. He explains, "In the 1960s, after her fifth child was born, my mother's doctor insisted she go on the Pill to help regulate her menstrual cycles. Dutifully she consulted our parish priest, and was told in no uncertain terms that recourse to the Pill was forbidden under any circumstance." His mother complied with religious regulations until the next hemorrhage, when she finally began taking the Pill, which brought some relief to her symptoms. None of this would have been discussed back then, of course. Later in life, it was mentioned only to Baumann's sisters. At the time, comments on the topic did not focus on health matters or reproductive choices. The author writes, "I do remember her complaining bitterly, in the proud way the Irish do, about women on the Pill who still presented themselves at the Communion rail." His mother slowly drifted away from Catholic practice, going only to weddings, baptisms, and funerals for years and then, eventually, she stopped going to church altogether. "She seemed to think," Baumann reflects, "that when it

65. W. L. Portier et al., "A Modus Vivendi: Sex, Marriage and the Church," *Commonweal*, December 27, 2011, https://www.commonwealmagazine.org/modus-vivendi, accessed July 19, 2016.

came to the church, you were all in or all out." This author may never have had to contemplate the Pill, but his story reveals the deeply entrenched ideas about gender and sex and the church's perceived authority over both.

Lessons issuing norms about sexuality and sexual behavior occurred in a wide range of circumstances, from overt statements to subtle inferences. Some may have required years of life experience to be grasped fully; others were clearly understood from the beginning. For the children growing up in Catholic households of the mid-twentieth century, this intimate, and essential, part of life was carefully regulated by religious authority inside and outside the home.

### Catholic Criteria for Kinship

Born Catholic. Catholic by birth. As I noted earlier, writers use language of genetic inheritance to link themselves to their tradition. Among my children's generation, the concept might be a harder sell. The simple religious affiliation of one's parents no longer guarantees a lifelong Catholic identity, at least not a satisfying one. For many authors who depict mid-twentieth-century Catholic life, though, the basic fact of a family's Catholicism had lifelong implications. The most poignant examples of this surface not in memories of church participation during childhood, but rather in reflections on growing distance from the church during adulthood. According to some, moving away from the faith requires more than foregoing Mass and ignoring religious teachings; it means abandoning one's family. To be a son or daughter, it was assumed and expected that the boys and girls, men and women in these narratives would be Catholic. As noted in the introduction, Alice McDermott describes the centrality of religion to her family's identity: "We were Catholics as inevitably as we were ourselves: the McDermott family on Emily Avenue, and with about as much self-consciousness and, it seemed, volition."[66] She claims that Catholicism was one of the McDermotts' distinguishing traits. It was barely chosen and rarely examined. This religious environment leaves a deep impression as adults find their own way in this changing world.

Author Garry Wills shares the deep connection to his church established early in life. Even after a lifetime of analysis and some harsh criticism of that church in his professional writing, he explains he could never leave it. He writes, "I am a born Catholic. I have never stopped going to Mass, saying the rosary, studying the Gospels. I have never even considered leaving the church. I would lose my faith in God before losing my faith in it."[67] Failed and flawed as it might be for Wills, he recognizes that it is essentially rooted in his DNA and will always be his.

Marianna De Marco Torgovnick (b. 1949) expresses the strong connection between faith and family in her memoir. In a rebellious move that her teenage friends could hardly believe, she decided never to return to church after receiving the sacrament of confirmation. While her peers always believed she wouldn't last away, she stuck to that decision. Still, moments in life call her back. She writes, "I returned to that church only for one uncle's funeral, then another's, and then, just last year, for my father's. It wasn't the church that drew me. It was the family, the way that tradition expresses itself most for Italian Americans."[68] Belonging to her Italian-American family means being Catholic and going to their church. Torgovnick cites Richard Rodriguez's description of Catholics as "a people of the 'we'" and reflects on the power of that in her own life: "When Italian American daughters rebel, their 'I-ness' comes through loud and strong—but so too does their remem-

---

66. Alice McDermott, "Confessions of a Reluctant Catholic," 12.

67. Garry Wills, *Why I Am a Catholic* (Boston: Houghton Mifflin, 2002), 13.

68. Marianna De Marco Torgovnick, *Crossing Ocean Parkway* (Chicago: University of Chicago Press, 1994), 153.

brance of the 'we.' They feel the lure of family and community—the thrill of self-sacrifice."[69] The tradition has a powerful draw. For her, it's part of being her uncles' niece and her father's daughter. Even as she has moved away from it, she feels the pull of it through her family's deep ties.

This connection between Catholic tradition and family belonging takes different forms among these texts. For David Plante, it involves practice and sacrament: "Away on my own, I had stopped going to Mass, but back home with my parents I had to go with them. I kept from them that I hadn't been to Mass for a year as I kept from them that I had also stopped going to confession."[70] While on his own, he admits, he has fallen away from participation in regular Catholic ritual, but when he is with his parents, he feels drawn back into the religion. For him, being with his parents includes going to Mass. He does not even entertain the idea of informing them that he has abandoned religious practice. Instead, he indicates how he falls seamlessly into the role of their son next to them in the pew.

Patricia Hampl intimates that going along with her parents' religious devotion proved a more difficult challenge. Feeling the enormous pressure of her parents, in her late teens she finally finds the nerve to tell her father the truth about her decision to stop going to Mass. She recalls the Sunday morning when he casually asked her which Mass she would be attending. She narrates, "'I'm not going,' I say, 'I'm not going to Mass anymore.' I can't believe I've said it, this thing that has gnawed at me for months, years." Finally liberated from her secret, she faces a daunting scene: "There is a god-like silence. . . . 'Your choice,' he says, managing to say the two bitter words without leaving a fingerprint of emotion on them." As if that response were not difficult enough for the young woman to bear,

69. Ibid.
70. Plante, *American Ghosts*, 128.

she recalls the follow-up: "We never speak of it again. Though my mother, the voice of the marriage, says a week later in the kitchen, 'You broke your father's heart.'"[71] This kind of attachment between a family's Catholic practice and a daughter's filial obligation puts an eighteen-year-old in a tough position. Even if she does intend to abandon the church, she faces the heart-wrenching disappointment of her parents. When later, as an adult, she decides to visit Catholic pilgrimage sites and reports this news to her parents, the response remains consistent: "Later in the kitchen, the Voice gives me the word: 'Your father is so proud of you.'"[72] The switch from parental disappointment to parental pride directly correlates with Catholic participation.

As I reflect on my own "genetic inheritance" of this religious tradition, I recognize that my parents probably never considered leaving their church or raising their children without Catholicism. It had always been, and would always be, their faith. Despite such loyalty, at no time did they ever articulate their expectation that we would do the same. I suspect that they hoped we would continue as Catholics—this faith had offered them a longtime spiritual home, after all—but ultimately, it was our choice whether we pursued religious practice. As a parent, I see that my choice takes on new significance. Curiously, while my husband is no less Catholic than I, no less connected to the same type of religious upbringing I experienced, and remains absolutely committed to raising our children in the church, I perceive a different level of expectation, as a daughter and mother, to integrate faith into family life. Catholic kinship seems to perpetuate many of the gender dynamics from an earlier generation: the parents offer a united force for the family's religious identity and the fathers confirm the importance of a child's Catholic upbringing, but ultimately, mothers accept the

71. Hampl, *Virgin Time*, 17.
72. Ibid.

responsibility for passing on the religious heritage. As it turns out, this implication is deeply rooted in the church's message. Pope Francis himself offered his reflection on the topic during a Mass upon the Feast Day of St. Timothy, who wrote that the saint's own faith came through his grandmother and mother. The pope takes the interpretation one step further in his homily: "It is the path chosen by Jesus. He wanted to have a mother: the gift of faith comes to us through women, as Jesus came to us through Mary."[73] This places me in a long line of Catholic women who have borne this responsibility, but it seems that tendency is changing. In an opinion piece on CNN's website, anchor Carol Costello takes up this topic and looks to scholar Kathleen Cummings' interpretation of a recent Pew survey. Cummings explains, "For the first time in history, young Catholic women are more disengaged than their male counterparts. . . . That is a huge, important shift. If you don't have women, you lose the children."[74] I certainly cannot speak for any other Catholic woman of my generation, but I am left to wonder if the gendered nature of my experience might resonate with others my age and, further, how church membership might change in the coming decades as women move away from their centuries-old role of passing on the tradition.

Returning to the literature of the mid-twentieth century, readers might notice that alongside dramatic departures and difficult discussions, some authors frame this deep connection between family life and Catholic faith another way: as a first language. Once again, Alice McDermott captures well a perception of the pro-

73. Ann Schneible, "Women Are Irreplaceable in Passing on the Faith, Pope Says," *Catholic News Agency*, January 26, 2015, http://www.catholicnewsagency.com/news/women-are-irreplaceable-in-passing-on-the-faith-pope-says-21135/, accessed July 27, 2016.

74. Carol Costello, "Pope Francis, Women Are Waiting," CNN, September 11, 2015, http://www.cnn.com/2015/09/10/opinions/costello-women-in-church/index.html, accessed July 27, 2016.

foundly defining nature of Catholicism among those "born into it." She describes a time of her own adult rebellion from the church, which coincided with her development as a novelist. Her writing life, she explains, began to reveal "a healthy sense of inevitability." Once she committed herself to a story, it was hers to finish, "come what may." This leads to another poignant realization: "Catholicism, I began to see, was also mine, inextricably mine, the fabric of my life and thoughts. It was the native language of my spirit, the way in which I had from the beginning thought about faith." She acknowledges that there are many other languages for faith and even admits that some might be better than her Catholicism, but they are not hers. She writes, "I would have to live another life entirely in order to know them and feel them as deeply as I knew and felt my Catholic faith."[75] Even as she knows that choice abounds, McDermott articulates the inescapability of an inherited Catholicism that shapes her world.

Mary Gordon identifies this experience of language through her fiction in the short story "Temporary Shelter." The protagonist, Joseph, and his mother, Helen, live with the Meyers family, who hired Helen as a housekeeper and caretaker. Even though Dr. Meyers had hoped to hire an Irish woman, he settles for a Pole because in the end, according to him, it was only important "that the person who would be caring for his daughter shared the Faith." Joseph reflects on the man's use of this term: "The way Dr. Meyers said 'The Faith' made Joseph feel sorry for him. It was a clue, if anyone was looking for clues, that he had not been born a Catholic, and all those things that one breathed in at Catholic birth, he'd had to learn, as if he had been learning a new language."[76] Through her character, Mary Gordon depicts the perceived religious inheritance that simply ac-

75. Alice McDermott, "Confessions of a Reluctant Catholic," 15.

76. Gordon, "Temporary Shelter," in *The Stories of Mary Gordon* (New York: Pantheon, 2006), 278.

companies the fact of being born of two particular people during the mid-twentieth century. The language of Catholicism imparted through DNA seems beyond the reach of any convert, no matter how devout.

American Catholicism of the 1940s, '50s, and '60s certainly included catechism and confession, but as the narratives in this chapter illustrate, so too was it shaped by home icons and the click of rosary beads. In some cases, this familiarity provided comfort and stability. In others, it imposed undesirable demands. Regardless of their reactions, authors construct in their literature a Catholicism that enveloped them—a cultural experience as well as one of faith and practice. In the next chapter, we shift our focus from inside the home to just outside it. As noted, families had been introducing children to ethnic practices, but in the meantime surrounding communities were actively contributing to the development of ethnic Catholicism. By focusing on the neighborhood, I consider yet another context for Catholic life.

# CHAPTER 4

# In Death, as in Life, We Will Be Irish

## Constructing Identities in the Community

The start of official religious education for my rising first-grade daughter at our parish created some anxiety, mostly for her, but maybe for her parents, too. She would be attending a relatively new intensive summer program that met for eight consecutive weekdays from eight in the morning until three in the afternoon. It began the Monday after the last day of public school and took place in the classrooms of the recently closed parish school. The only person who we knew would be there was the rising fourth-grader who lived directly across the street and had been through it once before. This brought some comfort. On the first day, though, everyone could relax: there were two of her public-school kindergarten classmates in her group of nine students. Familiar faces brought instant reassurance. This was going to be fine.

Most readers would not find anything striking about my daughter's experience. Children usually feel nervous about starting something new and relieved when friends are unexpectedly involved. If this moment were assessed from the perspectives of mid- twentieth-century Catholic children depicted in memory and story, though, most aspects would feel unfamiliar. The widely accepted norm of public schooling for Catholic children might have seemed unusual. Edward A. Malloy (b. 1941) remembers the public school adjacent to his own St. Anthony's in Washington, D.C., in the 1940s: "Other than that shared use of outdoor space, we had absolutely no contact during the school day with the public school students. Our neighborhood was so overwhelmingly Catholic that I remember having discussions with my peers about why these other kids had not yet discovered the truth."[1] Catholic peers from the public school might be the first distinction noted by those earlier generations. Further, because everyone they knew was Catholic, there would be few surprises at any church program or function. They would have undoubtedly expected their kindergarten pals and known the rest of the children there from the neighborhood. After all, during those decades, the neighborhood had been built around the parish, and everyone knew just about everyone who was part of it.

The neighborhood—its intimate spaces between home and church—emerges as a crucial context for the religious development of Catholic children during the 1940s, '50s, and '60s. In what appeared a homogeneous community, kids felt like the whole world was Catholic. If there were exceptions, they were known. The ethnic and socioeconomic dimensions that distinguished certain neighborhoods contributed to their communities' character and sometimes became linked with the faith in children's minds. In both autobiographical and fictional stories, writers depict a world where one could be surrounded by Catholics and be claimed by an ethnic group. Within cultural Catholicism, neighborhoods largely determined a person's connection to her religious heritage.

1. Edward. A. Malloy, CSC, *Monk's Tale: The Pilgrimage Begins, 1941–1975* (Notre Dame, Ind.: University of Notre Dame Press, 2009), 40.

As I focus on community origins in this chapter, I trace the effects of these places themselves. In reviewing the literature, I consider four emphases: (1) the insular nature of and the physical indicators within neighborhoods made Catholic membership an inevitable characterizing feature; (2) the neighborhood assigned an ethnic identity that naturally accompanied a Catholic one; (3) particular ethnic identities involved certain norms and expectations in Catholic life; and (4) ethnic religious character had class ramifications that would apply to this generation in complicated ways as they grew up. Just as they represent having internalized the rules and obligations of the church and having genetically inherited their Catholicism, authors suggest that neighborhood membership and ethnic affiliation permeated religious experience.

### Geography, Demography, and Inevitable Associations

In an autobiographical essay, Mary Gordon vividly depicts the insular nature of her childhood surroundings. She writes, "One could be, at least in the time when I was growing up, a Catholic in New York and deal only in the most superficial ways with anyone non-Catholic. . . . Real life, the friendships, the feuds, the passions of proximate existence, took place in the sectarian compound, a compound like any other, with its secrets—a secret language, secret customs."[2] Conveying the compound-like quality, Gordon emphasizes that her childhood community completely surrounded her with Catholics. They were the only people with whom she or her family associated, and she recognized herself as a true member of this clan. The place itself issued customs and rites, and she was socialized into its habits. Now distanced from that neighborhood, Gordon acknowledges how peculiar it must have seemed to

2. Gordon, *Good Boys and Dead Girls*, 164.

those outside it. She reflects on how the secretive nature of its ways "must have been very menacing at worst or at the best puzzling to the outside world." Nevertheless, it characterized her youth, and she perceives herself a product of it.[3]

In her memoir, *Virgin Time*, Patricia Hampl narrates her realization of how a specific place had changed her forever. She recalls this experience as an adult: "I took a long walk through my neighborhood, which is also the neighborhood of my childhood and of everything that made me Catholic to begin with."[4] She describes the critical markers of this space and the language it produced. "The parishes of the diocese, unmarked and ghostly as they were," she recalls, "posted borders more decisive than the street signs we passed on our way to St. Luke's grade school, or later, walking in the other direction to the girls-only convent high school."[5] Such borders naturally yielded divisions that defined one's origin. "We were like people with dual citizenship," writes Hampl. "I lived on Linwood Avenue but I *belonged* to St. Luke's. That was the lingo." She reflects on the amusing result of this lingo. Narrating an interaction at a school dance, Hampl recounts, "'I'm from Holy Spirit,' the boy said, as if he'd been beamed in to stand by the tepid Cokes and tuna sandwiches and the bowls of sweating potato chips on the refreshments table. Parish members did not blush to describe themselves as being 'from Immaculate Conception.' Somewhere north, near the city line, there was a parish frankly named Maternity of Mary."[6] Recalling these identifiers, phrases that would immediately place a person where she "belonged," Hampl conveys the complete lack of self-reflexivity in the use of such language. The Cath-

3. Ibid. For a scholarly consideration of sacred place, see Belden Lane, "Giving Voice to Place: Three Models for Understanding American Sacred Space," *Religion and American Culture* 11, no. 1 (2001): 53–81.

4. Hampl, *Virgin Time*, 39.

5. Ibid., 41.

6. Ibid., 42.

olic parishes had become part of everyday vocabulary and closely implicated every person who hailed from them with the narratives of the church and its faith.

Such normative description was not limited to Minnesota. Alice McDermott refers to this tendency in her novel *Child of My Heart* when her narrator's parents realize that their New York pasts match closely with those of some new friends. In reporting their efforts to establish the connection, the narrator reflects on the curious habit of tracing their stories "to the names of Catholic parishes, as if no identity of friend or cousin or coworker could be truly established without first determining where she had been baptized or schooled or married or (their phrase again) buried from—no landmark of their histories truly confirmed without the name of the nearest church to authenticate it."[7] The places of their youths disclosed these individuals' identities for McDermott's characters, and both the sites and the residents along with them had become inescapably connected to the Catholic parishes. Adults felt defined by their relationship to churches of their past. Catholicism was a key element of their life stories, not just the faith of their childhood.

John Bernard Ruane's experience in the southwest part of Chicago was nothing different. He recalls that when he met someone new and was asked where he was from, "the initial answer was always 'Bede's.' Our home was our parish and anyone blurting out 'Bede's,' or 'Dennis' or 'Redeemer' understood who you were and where you lived."[8] The name of a saint or a phrase describing Jesus, the nicknames for the particular church, were easy ways to place a person, literally and figuratively.

Scholar John McGreevy points out the historical and sociological foundation for this powerful connection between parish and neigh-

7. Alice McDermott, *Child of My Heart* (New York: Farrar, Straus and Giroux, 2002), 144–45.
8. Ruane, *Parish the Thought*, 6.

borhood. He notes that Catholics of the mid-twentieth century worked hard to purchase their homes, and those homes were near their church. That church itself was rooted in a particular place. McGreevy explains, "Crucially, the parish was immovable.... Catholic parishes and their property were registered in the name of the diocese and by definition served the people living within the parish boundary. Even Catholic parishes defined by nationality tended to have geographical boundaries as well, and worked on the assumption that the vast majority of church members would live in the immediate neighborhood." This yielded tremendous effect: "Catholic neighborhoods were created, not found.... For parishioners, the neighborhood *was* all-Catholic, given the cultural ghetto constructed by the parish."[9] It was such a widely accepted reality that, as McGreevy details, "through the 1950s, advertisements in Philadelphia, Buffalo, and Chicago newspapers often listed available apartments and homes by *parish*—'Holy Redeemer 2 Flat' or 'Little Flower Bungalow'—instead of using community names."[10] In many places during these decades, the neighborhood was the parish and the parish was the neighborhood.[11]

Madeleine Blais, on the other hand, might have connected a bit more with my daughter's earlier-mentioned experience than some of these others. While her New England town had a parish, Catholic life for children was a little different there than in many other Northeastern communities. The church did not have a parochial school, so she attended public school with the other Catholics in the neighborhood. Also, they did have regular contact with non-Catholics, but there would be no surprises as to which cate-

9. John T. McGreevy, *Parish Boundaries: The Catholic Encounter with Race in the Twentieth-Century Urban North* (Chicago: University of Chicago Press, 1996), 19, 20.

10. Ibid., 21.

11. For more on this deep connection between urban neighborhoods and parish community, see Gerald Gamm, *Urban Exodus: Why the Jews Left Boston and the Catholics Stayed* (Cambridge, Mass.: Harvard University Press, 1999).

gory anyone might claim. She explains, "In our town the divisions were simple: you could be young or old, male or female, Catholic or Protestant." This division had its starkest example in Eileen O'Sullivan. Her house was the first stop on the walk home from school for the uphill patrol, the group of students who lived close enough not to take the bus and lived up the hill. "Eileen and Brian lived with their buttoned-down Yankee mother and their dashing Irish father, P. Pearce O'Sullivan," writes Blais. "Mrs. O'Sullivan went to the Congregational Church on the hill across from our house: its leaves blew onto our lawn every autumn. Mr. O'Sullivan was Catholic, and he went to the Immaculate Heart of Mary, also in the center of town, along with our family."[12] So while Blais's younger self could connect to my daughter's public schooling and need for additional catechism education, the rest of her experience would likely seem foreign. She might question how my daughter did not already know exactly who was Catholic and who was not and the particular parish every person attended.

What really would have thrown young Blais for a loop would have been to learn that the summer after that introductory catechism session for my daughter at our church, that same daughter and our four-year-old son would actually attend Vacation Bible Camp at the Methodist church across the street from the parish. (The intensive Catholic religious instruction program was not available to my daughter that summer, since she was entering second grade, a sacrament year, and would have to do the more traditional weekly sessions.) In fact, it would be hard for my own younger self to believe such interdenominational participation could be possible. The Episcopalian church that sat only a few hundred yards from my childhood home seemed like a mysterious cave, and I never knew anyone who had entered it. The only evidence I

12. Blais, *Uphill Walkers*, 27.

had that people actually attended were the weekly lines of parked cars along the street on Sunday morning. I remember thinking that their drivers and passengers must come a long way to attend. Surely, these churchgoers were not "from around here." Dropping my children off at the surf-themed camp where they would be riding the waves of God's love, I was grateful for the few hours of engaged and positive summertime childcare and amazed at how distant my childhood perception of other denominations would be from my children's ecumenical experience of Christianity. My children might know which church is *their* church, but they also know it's not the only game in town. Most of the authors considered here depict a different understanding of religion in the neighborhood.

### Ethnic Expectations

Another implication that usually accompanied Catholic affiliation was an ethnic identity. Most people would not have been known simply as Catholic, but rather as Irish Catholic, Italian Catholic, or German Catholic, for example. We recall Claudia DeMonte, the artist from Astoria, Queens, considered in chapter 1, who claims, "The whole world was Italian to me." If you grew up in the Bensonhurst section of Brooklyn, like author Maria De Marco Torgovnick did, you were also likely to be Italian. Of course, depending on which street you lived, you could also be Irish or Jewish.[13] If you fell into the Italian or the Irish category, you were most definitely Catholic. Torgovnick describes the precise distinctions that persist among people from this neighborhood: "Jews are suspect but (the old Italian women admit) 'they make good husbands.' The Irish are okay, fellow Catholics, but not really 'like us'; they make bad husbands because they drink and gamble."[14] Us and them. Good and

13. A similarly homogeneous ethnic community is portrayed in Orsi, *The Madonna of 115th Street*.

14. Torgovnick, *Crossing Ocean Parkway*, 7.

bad. Even decades later, the divisions remain recognizable, according to Torgovnick. If you came from a certain place, you were likely to claim a certain ethnic heritage, and, depending on what that heritage was, your Catholicism could easily be assumed.

In some neighborhoods, the streets were not as homogeneous, with Irish and Italian families living side by side and Catholicism emanating from all corners. Maria Laurino recalls how the ethnic neighborhood could even serve as another Catholic classroom. She explains, "Religious instruction came from neighbors as well as nuns, and an early prayer I learned is still vivid in my memory. Our next-door neighbor, a kind but strict teacher and devout Irish Catholic who saw my religious upbringing as part of her duty, taught me this bedtime ditty."[15] She goes on to recite the prayer, which included the request that if she were to die, her soul be protected. Her memory reveals clearly distinguishable ethnicities; while she knew that her family was Italian American, she had no doubt that her neighbor was Irish American. Ethnic heritage was common knowledge.

This ethnic paradigm of either Irish or Italian in the Catholic neighborhoods proves to be a powerful standard for children in the mid-twentieth century. In fact, for some, it seemed they were the only groups who existed. In Mary Gordon's essay "Girl Child in a Women's World," she shows how deeply ingrained the link between these ethnic heritages and Catholic faith was throughout her youth. The connection was so strong, in fact, that an ethnic identity outside this norm made one's faith questionable. Gordon recalls her caretaker: "Although Mrs. Kirk's family traced their allegiance to the Church back for centuries, I found it unconvincing. They were neither Irish nor Italian like the other people in my parish."[16] If your identifiable ethnicity (and it seems ethnicity was always

15. Laurino, *Were You Always an Italian?*, 162.
16. Gordon, *Seeing through Places*, 63.

clearly marked) happened to fall into some category beyond Irish or Italian, it could mean that your Catholicism was suspect.

In recent theoretical work on ethnic identity in the United States, scholars have shown that this category and the defining criteria for different ethnicities constantly change and evolve as people construct them. American adults, particularly those with certain phenotypes, ultimately control their ethnic self-conceptions.[17] So, even though ethnicity might be perceived as an inherited trait, its character and effects have been created, predominantly, by those who claim it. What it means to be Italian American, for example, ultimately depends on how those who claim to be Italian American define it. This theoretical approach to ethnic identity offers an interesting lens for reading narratives about cultural Catholicism during the mid-twentieth century. Through their stories, authors depict the ethnic constructions they encountered as children. The stories themselves contribute to the ongoing evolution of those same ethnic identities by passing them on to a next generation of readers.

For the parents and grandparents hoping to maintain the immigrant church they had built, however, their ethnicity was nothing, if not clear, real, and longstanding. "Racial parishes," as they were known at the time, indicating a kind of blindness to peoples beyond European groups, were church communities established to serve specific ethnic populations through emphasis on original language and culture. These were prized by Catholics of the mid-century, and efforts to protect their community's homogeneity sometimes came at terribly high costs. This applied particularly

17. See Wendy F. Katkin, Ned C. Landsman, and Andrea Tyree, *Beyond Pluralism: The Conception of Groups and Group Identities in America* (Urbana: University of Illinois Press, 1998); Werner Sollors, *Theories of Ethnicity: A Classical Reader* (Washington Square, N.Y.: New York University Press, 1996); Sollors, *The Invention of Ethnicity* (New York: Oxford University Press, 1988); Mary C. Waters, *Ethnic Options: Choosing Identities in America* (Berkeley: University of California Press, 1990).

to areas where African Americans were moving from the Southern states into Northern cities. Across the country, organized protests and even violent riots resulted when blacks moved into previously white areas, especially when integrated public-housing complexes were proposed for certain ethnic Catholic neighborhoods.[18] For African-American Catholics, this proved an especially painful reality: even their Catholic brothers and sisters, even in many cases Catholic priests, fought hard to keep them away. Ethnic affiliation within Catholicism showed its sinister side when it came to interracial—this time meaning black and white—relations. Several leaders, such as white Jesuit priests John LaFarge and William Markoe and black intellectual Thomas Wyatt Turner, worked hard to overcome challenges posed to African-American Catholics.[19] Their efforts effected change, but injustice inevitably persists.

The harsh reality of racism within American Catholicism casts a large shadow over the circumstances that children experienced during the mid-twentieth century. Perhaps adding to the unfair history, the fictional and autobiographical narratives I have encountered about this time include scarce mention of protests or riots. The authors themselves may have edited out such ugly ramifications of ethnic enclaves, but as the stories read, the racial tensions did not reach their neighborhoods. Children navigated the expectations and conflicts that emerged from their local sites and struggled to discern how these applied to themselves. Their published stories perpetuate the understood implications of a European ethnic lineage.

So what might readers today discover about certain mid-twentieth-century European-descended ethnic peoples in this litera-

18. See McGreevy, *Parish Boundaries*.

19. For more, see Cyprian Davis, *The History of Black Catholics in the United States* (New York: Crossroad, 1990); McGreevy, *Parish Boundaries*; M. Shawn Copeland, ed., *Uncommon Faithfulness: The Black Catholic Experience* (Maryknoll, N.Y.: Orbis, 2009).

ture? It depends on the source. A range from deep resentment to fond nostalgia characterizes the treatment of ethnic heritage and Catholic upbringing in general. As evidenced so far, stories about growing up Catholic tend to focus on the Irish and Italian examples, though other ethnic groups certainly established firm roots in American Catholicism. Franco-American David Plante might take issue with the lopsided attention given these groups. Still, to get a little sample of the typically represented experience, I briefly profile the resentment/nostalgia spectrum for Irish Catholics and Italian Catholics in depictions of ethnic heritage.

For some, an Irish heritage could feel like a curse. It imposed a burden of negativity that felt heavy and hard. Patricia Hampl narrates her fraught relationship with her mother, who proudly claimed her Irish ancestry. Hampl had a hard time finding much redeemable about this connection. She writes, "The Irish side was soggy with spite—dashed hopes, missed turns, bad bets, rotten deals, deep sighs—given over finally to a swoon known as trust in the good Lord."[20] It was a way of seeing the world that made one a victim and that made faith a byproduct. Clearly, this author does not communicate much fondness for her Irish roots. She occupies one side of a wide range.

On the other, Martha Manning portrays an Irish experience that feels almost buoyant and optimistic. She claims, "In death, as in life, we will be Irish—surrounded by our friends and family, by the music we love, by grand stories inflated with every telling, by drinking and eating (in that order), by the free flow of tears, and by one of the greatest comforts in grief: a couple of straight shots of laughter."[21] Here, at the heart of being Irish is community and camaraderie within inevitable suffering and loss. It is a solace. Garry Wills likewise remembers a jovial spirit among his mother's

20. Patricia Hampl, *The Florist's Daughter* (Orlando, Fla.: Harcourt, 2007), 164.
21. Manning, *Chasing Grace*, 206.

relatives, particularly in comparison to his father's non-Catholic side of the family. He writes, "It was the Catholic part of my life— the Irish Catholic side of the family—that was most supportive and stimulating." He continues the comparison: "The Irish side . . . was all love and little improving. The Collinses had their faults, some recognized (the drink), some not (the racism), but they made children feel instantly at home."[22] Such an appealing Irish character—and characters—made their way into Hollywood depictions of the time, as well. John Ford, director of *The Quiet Man* released in 1952, brings to the screen a bucolic, Catholic, and communal existence in the protagonist's native Ireland. When John Wayne's Sean Thornton, an American, courts the Irish Mary Kate Danaher, played by Maureen O'Hara, viewers fall in love with the characters and their context. Narrated by the local Irish priest, the film brings to life a Motherland that Irish Americans romanticized.

Between dark depictions and romantic approach lie the majority of Irish Catholic attitudes. Alice McDermott shares a playful kind of resentment, noting the firm, even unrelenting, grasp this heritage can claim on a person. Explaining the subject matter of her writing, which tends toward Irish Catholic characters, she says, "I really think probably that Catholicism has me by the throat and the soul more than Irishness, but that might be saying the same thing. They may be one and the same."[23] The inherent connection between ethnicity and religion exert unquestionable power over her life and her writing.

Monica Wood offers a fairly neutral, if nostalgic, approach that includes a shared common past with the assurance of bright futures. She recalls, "Like most Irish Catholic families in 1963, mine

22. Wills, *Why I Am a Catholic*, 13–14.

23. Tom Smith, *Transcript of the Book Show* (1992), New York State Writers Institute, 1998, http://www.albany.edu/writers-inst/olv2n3.html#mcdermott, accessed March 4, 2006.

had a boiled dinner on Sundays after Mass and salmon loaf on Fridays. We had pictures of Pope John and President John and the Sacred Heart of Jesus hung over our red couch." She describes the many ethnic groups that made her small town of Mexico, Maine, home and the easy way they coexisted: "Though our elders in Mexico—who spoke French, or Italian, or Lithuanian, or English with a lilt—cherished their cultural differences, which were deep and mysterious and preserved in family lore, what bound us, the children . . . was the future we shared, the promise of a long and bountiful life."[24] Wood's Irishness includes particular habits and markers along with a shared bond. It unified one generation without limiting the next. Readers who grew up in similar circumstances as these authors might find something in each of their depictions that feels familiar. The wide spectrum might even apply to a singular person, with little contradiction. Such is the nature of ethnic Catholic life.

The same applies to Italian American experience. A scan of the spectrum might find one reader relating to all parts, even as they seemingly negate each other. Marianna De Marco Torgovnick shares a damaging image that she has associated with her ethnic past. She writes, "When I think of Italian American girlhood, I think about being parceled and bound. I think of the little brides of Christ, all lined up in identical white veils and dresses, waiting to be confirmed at age thirteen."[25] The harsh imposition of ethnic religion defines her memory. "Parceled and bound," young Italian Catholics could suffer severe restrictions as a result of their upbringing.

Far removed from this austere image, author Jay Parini (b. 1948) shares a markedly different perception of Italian American life: "I'm by nature a village person, which is to say I adore the feeling of community that can be had only on a neighborhood scale. This, I like to think, is part of my Italian heritage: a world in which family

24. Wood, *When We Were the Kennedys*, xvi, xvii.
25. Torgovnick, *Crossing Ocean Parkway*, 151.

and community were everything."[26] Much like the Irish examples, attitudes range from disparagement to celebration. Ethnicity could be either a source of repression or an opportunity for connection. Again, in most cases, recollections fall somewhere in between.

In a more neutral tone, Helen Barolini (b. 1925) recalls the confusing task of claiming her nationality on school and camp forms. "I never knew what to put: was I American or Italian? . . . Though the records said I was American, from the start my soul wasn't persuaded."[27] Again, much like McDermott's Irish connection, Barolini feels claimed by Italianness without a choice in the matter, but her tone conveys a loving resignation with little hint of bitterness.

In her own nostalgic move, Claire Gaudiani describes an ethnic life that forged bonds from a shared culture, even as it allowed for pragmatic planning about life ahead. She explains, "Family values were Italian; civic values were American." The key was the way they could work together: "For us, the focus on faith, food and family, especially tenderness to children and the poor, were as strong as the focus on premier achievement in American society—Italian Catholic spirituality in the context of American striving." It offered a happy balance whereby the gift of community allowed space for achievement.

Reflecting on this powerful aspect of their pasts, authors confirm that ethnic Catholicism could feel like a binding constraint or a loving embrace. I suspect for some, it fluctuated between these on any given day. Regardless of one's emotional response to these categories, though, certain truths about what typified these identities emerge in this literature.

---

26. Parini, "Amalfi Days," in *Beyond the Godfather*, 109.

27. Helen Barolini, *Chiaroscuro: Essays of Identity* (Madison: University of Wisconsin Press, 1999), 107.

*Implications and Norms of Ethnic*
*Constructions*

To be Irish or Italian for Catholics in the 1940s, '50s, and '60s meant more than a label on a form or mere membership in a group. These identities issued norms and expectations particular to each heritage, a set of characteristics that shaped religious perspective. Once again, neglecting other ethnic communities that had major impacts on American Catholicism, I do limit my examples to the widely available Irish and Italian depictions that dominate the literature. In memory and story, writers show how ethnic connections issued standards for religious experience.

To begin consideration of the Irish experience of Catholicism in the mid-twentieth-century United States, one must first acknowledge the intimate link to the clergy.[28] From Mary Gordon's New York to Richard Rodriguez's Sacramento, the institutional experience of the church in the United States was an Irish one.[29] Anyone who has seen the 1944 film *Going My Way* remembers a dashing Bing Crosby as the young Father Chuck O'Malley sent to replace the aging Father Fitzgibbons—a new generation of Irish to take over for the immigrant one that cleared a path. In real life beyond the big screen, this ethnic dynamic had a range of effects. First, it meant a certain comfort level for Irish Catholics in parish life and church involvement. It also meant a sense of loyalty to the institutional church. Helen Barolini remembers growing up Italian alongside the Irish. She describes her neighbor and friend Mary Ann Sheed

28. See Dolores Liptak, *Immigrants and Their Church* (New York: Macmillan, 1989); Olson, *Catholic Immigrants in America*, 15–46; James M. O'Toole, "'The Newer Catholic Races': The Varieties of Ethnic Catholicism," in *Militant and Triumphant: William Henry O'Connell and the Catholic Church of Boston, 1859–1944* (Notre Dame, Ind.: University of Notre Dame Press, 1992).

29. Richard Rodriguez, *Days of Obligation: An Argument with My Mexican Father* (New York: Viking, 1992), 191; Gordon, *Conversations with Mary Gordon*, 10.

and what she learned from their interactions. Barolini writes, "I could tell even then, that anyone Irish was more Catholic than I was. Mary Ann, in fact, took her uncle the priest very seriously; she took holy days and fasts very seriously; she did her penance devotedly; she could recite the 'laws' of the church with absolute certainty to tell me when I was afoul of them."[30] This relationship between the Irish and Italian Catholic communities would produce more serious divisions among the adults to be considered later in this chapter. From early in childhood, though, ethnic Catholics knew where they stood.

The element of death is another theme in narratives characterizing Irish-American Catholic practice. There is an old (albeit morbid) joke that calls the obituary section of the newspaper the Irish sports page—they followed this kind of news closely. Going to wakes—ritual viewings of the body and paying respects after a person has died—turns out to be a requirement for the Irish. In fact, missing the wake of a neighbor might even be considered a sin.

Martha Manning recalls the moment she learned she was Irish. It was at a relative's wake, her first. She recalls, "My cousin looked at me impatiently and insisted, 'Of course you're Irish: half the people here are O'Neills. You are an O'Neill.'" With this declaration from someone who seemed to have more information than she, Manning entered a whole new world of obligations. She continues, "I knew our family was very Catholic, but no one ever mentioned anything about Irish. Once my cousin convinced me that we were, in fact, Irish, I shuddered in anticipation of all the wakes in front of me."[31] With what she deems as little choice in the matter, Martha Manning resigns herself to a lifetime full of wakes.

Similarly, Dan Barry (b. 1958) recounts a conversation with his mother that confirms the obligatory nature of this practice. After

30. Barolini, *Chiaroscuro*, 12.
31. Manning, *Chasing Grace*, 202.

the death of a neighbor, Barry's mom feels tremendous guilt about having to miss the wake. The son shares, "The right thing, of course, would have been for the Barrys Up the Street to attend the wake. Although the families had not talked in years, there was still that bond among pioneers." When they do not attend, his mom feels the need to justify the absence: "My father's headaches had prevented the Barrys from getting to the funeral home on either of the two nights, my mother explained. I could tell that she felt uneasy about this; the Irish go to wakes, period. I could tell too that she wanted absolution from her eldest."[32] Sensing the severity of his mother's guilt, Barry recognizes her need for forgiveness because she missed the ritual event. Their descriptions illustrate how such a duty could be learned and perceived as unavoidable. As Irish Catholics, they were obliged and expected to perpetuate this practice. It came with the territory.

Also in the category of coming with the territory were guilt and silence. Ranging from minor lapses like missing a wake or confession to more conscious indulgences like achieving some worldly success, life, it seems, invited guilt for Irish Catholics. Perhaps this should come as no surprise during a time when children witnessed the "scrupulosity" of adults, intensely reviewing their behavior for the possibility of sin. For a community so connected to the institutional church, the detriment of sin and the importance of confession, guilt might seem a natural consequence. In Mary Gordon's novel *Spending*, a character says bluntly, "I suffer from Irish Catholic guilt about prosperity."[33] Given hard beginnings and economic challenges, Irish Catholics of the mid-twentieth century experienced deep discomfort when prosperity became even possible. The connection between suffering and holiness was deeply rooted. Certainly, one would never talk about such things, though. Silence

32. Dan Barry, *Pull Me Up: A Memoir* (New York: W. W. Norton, 2004), 203.
33. Gordon, *Good Boys and Dead Girls*, 211.

also governed. Readers might recognize the old Irish expression that usually followed any serious story or news: "Mind you, I've said nothing." Careful not to betray private matters, Irish Catholics kept things quiet.

These traits along with others led to a general understanding about proper conduct for Irish Catholics. In her novel *Child of My Heart*, Alice McDermott includes the expectations perceived by a young girl because of her ethnic, religious affiliation. Teresa, the novel's fifteen-year-old narrator, discovers that wealthy families on Long Island believe she would make an ideal babysitter. She explains her draw: "Pretty, intelligent, mature in speech although undeveloped physically (another plus), well immersed in my parents' old-fashioned Irish Catholic manners (inherited from their parents, who had spent their careers in service to this very breed of American rich), and best of all beloved by children and pets."[34] In a list of other appealing traits, she falls into a long lineage of Irish Catholics and, as such, would be expected to embody the etiquette for which they were known. Their historical economic position as immigrants contributed to their reputation of making good servants, of course, but their manners were understood to be a distinct result of their Irish Catholicism. By including this characterizing feature of her protagonist, McDermott emphasizes the roles and assumptions assigned to Irish Catholics. A teenager developing her own sense of self knows what others expect of her. Being Irish and Catholic involves much more than the sacraments; it issues character.

Italian Catholics have their own set of representative features depicted in memoir and fiction. Curiously, they are often first distinguished from the Irish Catholics who dominated the institutional church in the nineteenth and twentieth centuries. This dy-

34. Alice McDermott, *Child of My Heart*, 14.

namic determined much of the American Catholic milieu for those who grew up within it. Rudolph Giuliani (b. 1944) remembers the familiar rivalry: "In the late '40s and '50s, there was a tension between Irish Catholics and Italian Catholics, particularly among the priests and the nuns." For him, it even went beyond tension to a kind of hierarchy: "I think there was a sense and an attitude that Irish Catholics were better than Italian Catholics."[35] Superiority and resentment played important roles in the relationship between these ethnic communities. In Maria Laurino's *Were You Always an Italian?* she describes her grandmother's Italian piety in terms of how the Irish would have reacted. She writes, "The solitary chants of this solemn woman expressed a devotion that would have disturbed the American Irish Catholic hierarchy, which was suspicious of the southern Italian attachment to saints."[36] Learning the categorical features of each ethnic identity during childhood, Laurino recognizes that her grandmother's devotion represents a typical "southern Italian attachment to saints" and assumes that any reaction from the church would include criticism from Irish priests.

Giuliani's and Laurino's first-person accounts of the tension between the Irish hierarchy and the Italian laity concur with scholarship on this social dimension of the church in the United States.[37] Just as it would be hard to argue with the high numbers of Irish priests, so too would it be difficult to deny a devotion to the saints practiced among the Italian settlers and their descendants. Such affiliations often clashed. Laurino's narrative highlights the impact of this reality on a young girl. Many childhood depictions include

---

35. Rudolph Giuliani, "Outspoken Mayor, Battling Prosecutor," in *Growing Up Italian*, 234.

36. Laurino, *Were You Always an Italian?*, 158.

37. See Ronald H. Bayor, *Neighbors in Conflict: The Irish, Germans, Jews, and Italians of New York City, 1929–1941* (Baltimore: Johns Hopkins University Press, 1978); Liptak, "The Italian Challenge," in *Immigrants and Their Church*; Morris, *American Catholic*, 128–31.

a reference to a condemning authority looming over Italian Catholic ritual. Feast days and devotions would bring Italians into the streets for parades and rites. These kinds of religious demonstrations might threaten the more straitlaced Catholicism of the Irish and could embarrass those latter Catholics in front of their Protestant onlookers.

Italian Americans identify something else in their construction of an ethnic identity: good food enjoyed among many people. The event was more than a meal, though; it was understood as sacrament. In his work *Feeling Italian: The Art of Ethnicity in America*, scholar Thomas Ferraro articulates this sentiment using a term from a famed Italian-American cookbook author: "*Il sacro desco* translates as 'the sacred (dinner) table': a perfect phrase for what I have long experienced as Marian Catholic domestication of the Eucharist: in the classic Italian home the preparation of food is a sacred obligation undertaken daily on behalf of one's self, one's family, and one's intimates."[38] Beyond the simple preparation of the food, the experiences of cooking and enjoying the meal were connections with a community, and those interactions held the possibility for an encounter with God's grace.

This idea emerges in the writing of other self-identified Italian Americans. Claire Gaudiani writes, "Stories from my Italian ancestry and my life experience in my Italian American household made me a feminine misfit in my own generation."[39] Her role in the kitchen as a woman from an Italian family does not coincide with the women's liberation movement that affected so much of her American life. She recalls a conversation with a group of academic women colleagues at the end of a conference: "Conversation turned to weight, nutrition, cooking, and family traditions around

38. Thomas Ferraro, *Feeling Italian: The Art of Ethnicity in America* (New York: New York University Press, 2005), 185.
39. Gaudiani, "Of Cheese and Choices," 121.

food. I began to explain to my colleagues that in my family women cooked so well that food became 'the at home sacraments.'"[40] As she narrates this gendered expectation within an Italian community, she evokes religious language to convey the level of importance credited to food in its communal preparation and consumption. She senses confusion and concern from her companions. Those outside this ethnic religious heritage could not fully grasp the Catholic connection to the routine activity.

The sacramental metaphor offers another example of how Catholicism manifested itself for families and communities well outside the institutional church. Despite this domestic focus, it seems that the religious implications were strong enough for Alane Salierno Mason (b. 1964) to connect directly with more formal Catholicism. Like Dan Barry's mother, who considered missing a wake sinful for the Irish, Salierno Mason implies that disregarding the Italian way of eating calls for absolution. Her current career and lifestyle do not afford the opportunity to cook and eat the way she learned from her grandparents. She writes, "A dozen times a week I eat alone in a way that is against my cultural religion. Should I tell the priest, next time I go to confession, the number of times I took my food in vain?"[41] Her humorous interpretation of a commandment conveys the close association between her Italian and Catholic codes for living.

The topic of food and family raises another notable contrast between Irish and Italian Catholics for James Hannan, the product of a "mixed marriage." With the union of Hannan's first-generation Irish-American father and his first-generation Italian-American mother in the early part of the twentieth century came a whole host

40. Ibid.
41. Alane Salierno Mason, "The Exegesis of Eating," in *The Milk of Almonds: Italian American Women Writers on Food and Culture*, ed. Louise DeSalvo and Edvige Giunta (New York: Feminist Press at CUNY, 2002), 266.

of challenges.[42] Hannan writes that the tensions "were manifested in the respective families' approach to life and religion." He explains, "Family life for my Italian relatives was a ritual of togetherness. Every Sunday at noon, my parents, aunts, uncles, and cousins descended on my grandparents' house for Sunday gravy." Relatives would continue arriving throughout the day and stay into the night playing cards. When Hannan's Italian mother tries to institute this with the other side of the family, they do not quite catch on: "My mother's attempts to forge the same type of bond with my Irish grandparents were met with a combination of bemusement and discomfort. The Irish side of the family loved each other's company and had great times when they all got together. They just didn't get together all that often, and didn't really see the need to do so." For the most part, Hannan claims that he was able to balance the conflicting ethnic heritages, with occasional conflict: "Some days, I was Italian, others, Irish. (Imagine my dilemma when I had to choose a side when my Irish and Italian classmates gathered for the annual St. Patrick's Day brawl in the school courtyard.)"[43] In the end he learns to appreciate the richness of a blended Irish-Italian Catholicism.

I vividly recall many intense discussions during my own Catholic grade-school years about ethnic heritage. At the time it seemed particularly cool that I could claim 100 percent Irishness, with every one of my ancestors (allegedly) tracing back to that Motherland. Some of my friends could do the same. A few others were "purely" Italian, and lots more claimed a blend with maybe German or Polish in the mix. We had no real idea what significance any of this had, but we liked claiming membership among a certain people. As my children grow up, they might associate their Irish heritage

42. For more on these interethnic marriages see Moses, *An Unlikely Union*.
43. James Hannan, "A Mixed Marriage," *Commonweal*, December 10, 2014, https://www.commonwealmagazine.org/blog/mixed-marriage, accessed July 19, 2016.

with our annual pilgrimage to Scranton for the St. Patrick's Day Parade and the different shades of green that have collected in their wardrobes as a result. The story of the saint and the popular viewing location in front of the cathedral (we rarely make it to the Mass that precedes the parade) might link this day to its religious origins in their minds. With each generation, that immigrant experience recedes into history, leaving the nostalgic vestiges of a cultural inheritance.

## Class Implications Then and Now

With ethnic dimensions largely influencing the specifics of Catholic practice during the mid-twentieth century, this proximity to immigrant status included another important facet: social and economic class. Even within insular neighborhoods, children witnessed the developments of these relationships among the adults. Mary Gordon describes the up-close view afforded in her parish: "Anachronistically limited, its hierarchies clear, its loyalties assumed and stated and then in practice always undermined, it has at its center issues of money. You learned from the parish how the watermarks of class and privilege work."[44] While kids might not have realized it, the parish could teach lessons about economic status and its power alongside church catechism. Once again, for many, this had clear-cut ethnic dimensions. Maria Laurino takes this characterization of the parish even further by detailing the consequence of class distinctions for her own family. She writes, "The people my parents knew from the town of Millburn, the Italian Americans from the old neighborhood, sat in the back rows, veiled heads bowed, fingering rosary beads. These ladies in mournful black, vestiges of a nineteenth-century southern Italian culture, understood the social order as intimately as their prayers." Laurino

44. Gordon, *Good Boys and Dead Girls*, 164.

depicts the starkly ethnic class divisions that occurred inside the church itself: "The wealthy Irish-American parishioners, the majority in our church, wore bright prints and self-assured smiles, and mingled with each other in the front pews." Far removed from the front-row families but not quite identifying with those in the back, her family faced a dilemma: "Where did we fit in? Probably somewhere in between, in those middle rows where we sat by ourselves. The equality we were all supposed to experience in the eyes of God never reached those pews; the working-class women in the back accepted their place and remained there week after week."[45] Reflecting on the circumstances of her youth from a distance, the author portrays a situation that everyone accepted and lived. What becomes clear is that these levels of social status served only as a warmup for what some would find outside the parish. The conditions of advantage only increased when one glanced beyond these insular communities to a larger "America." Rita Ciresi represents this situation poignantly when her fictional character Lisa recalls a performance during elementary school. She describes the scene: "We stood as fifth-graders on the front steps of the Hartford capitol two weeks before election day and sang, 'Buon giorno, mio caro.' To a group of dark-suited state senators, who felt obliged to show their appreciation of Italian-American culture with a polite round of Protestant applause."[46] Her sarcastic tone about the patronizing response to the concert reveals the clear separation perceived between the young Italian Catholics on stage and the American Protestant men in charge. While the Irish may have had a leg up on the Italians, Catholics from all ethnic communities had their work cut out for them if they intended to move beyond their respective group's limitations.

The generation who came of age during the 1940s, '50s, and '60s

45. Laurino, *Were You Always an Italian?*, 164.
46. Ciresi, *Pink Slip*, 86.

occupied a unique position as American Catholics. Most of them were the descendants of immigrants, not immigrants themselves, and therefore encountered different conditions that allowed for a new relationship to ethnic identity.[47] Marianna De Marco Torgovnick emphasizes the distinct nature of her experience when compared to those who preceded her. She reflects on stories about an immigrant past and determines, "These stories nourished me—but they are the stories of my parents' and grandparents' generation. What I tell here is different from the story of arrival. It is the story of assimilation—one that Italian Americans of my generation are uniquely prepared to tell, and that females need to tell most of all."[48] Her generation—the one that witnessed its parents and grandparents struggle to make it in the United States and that has achieved success by American standards on its own—is poised to narrate assimilation. She reveals the key to this process: education. Higher education afforded opportunities to move beyond ethnic enclaves and achieve success outside the Catholic community.

Of course, mid-twentieth-century Catholics faced challenges not only from a secular (or Protestant) America that existed outside the neighborhood, but also from the expectations set within their communities. As Torgovnick notes, the pursuit of education could threaten one's connection to her childhood home, and not all family members liked this possibility. She writes, "My own mother could not understand my desire to go to college, thinking that I should instead become a secretary. . . . She rightly sensed (I see now in retrospect) that college would remove me from her

47. See Peter Kivisto, *Incorporating Diversity: Rethinking Assimilation in a Multicultural Age* (Boulder, Colo.: Paradigm, 2005); Kivisto, Dag Blanck, and Swenson Swedish Immigration Research Center, *American Immigrants and Their Generations: Studies and Commentaries on the Hansen Thesis after Fifty Years* (Urbana: University of Illinois Press, 1990); Rubén G. Rumbaut and Alejandro Portes, eds., *Ethnicities: Children of Immigrants in America* (Berkeley: University of California Press, 2001).

48. Torgovnick, *Crossing Ocean Parkway*, x.

world."[49] Expected to remain within the confines of the Catholic community, this generation's members received resistance when they took steps to go outside it. The parents and grandparents, the immigrants to whom Torgovnick referred, perceived the threat of education to their community. Mary Gordon concurs, sharing how this applied within the Irish world as well: "The more you learned, the more likely you were to leave home."[50] While not every family opposed such ambition, education would provide opportunities for ethnic Catholics that had not been enjoyed in the previous generation and that would expand their worlds well beyond the neighborhoods, for better and for worse, according to their elders.

If one could gather the nerve to make a run for American higher education, she had to convince the people within that world that she was worthy. Madeleine Blais remembers the terrible disappointment of being denied admission to Smith College. Her admissions interview was her clearest indication that she didn't have what it took. She writes, "What did I say that day that made me so deeply unappealing? Could it have been my suffocating earnestness? . . . Did I overemphasize the Catholic aspects of my education, which is to say, did I mention them at all? . . . Maybe it had been wrong to check the financial aid box, to tip the institution off to the depth of my financial need. All I know is that I have never felt so deeply invisible in all my life."[51] Regretting her attempts at false eloquence and her references to marching in the St. Patrick's Day parade, Blais encounters the harsh reality of making her way in a new educational realm.

Still, there was hope for many after 1960. The election of a Roman Catholic president assured the Irish, at least, that their people were making inroads. The same author shares her thoughts: "To the Blais family, the Kennedy White House was proof that we had

49. Ibid., 118.
50. Gordon and Bennett, *Conversations with Mary Gordon*, 10.
51. Blais, *Uphill Walkers*, 143.

arrived. . . . The whole nation had been shrunk to something small-er and more manageable, to parish. One of ours was at the helm."[52] This proved that possibility existed, even if routine interactions or college applications did not go their way immediately. The future seemed promising.

The stark contrast between an ethnic background and an ad-vanced education in the United States emerges powerfully in an es-say by John Agresto (b. 1946). He recalls bringing friends from grad-uate school to have dinner with his "very Italian grandmother" and the awkward exchanges these shared meals could generate. He nar-rates one visit: "Looking at the woman my grandmother began the quiz: 'You Italian?' (The young woman was nearly six foot, blonde, with green eyes, but Grandma was never much of a noticer.) 'No.' 'You Irish?' 'No.' 'You Jewish?' 'No.' 'You Portuguese?' 'No. I guess I'm part German, part Scandinavian, maybe some Russian, mostly just a mix of things.'" Apparently, the visiting woman realized that she had to offer some kind of answer to the question. This, howev-er, did not satisfy the grandmother. Agresto shares the matriarch's response: "Downcast eyes, turned head. My grandmother then said softly: 'How terrible not to be somebody.'"[53] It's a striking image: the young woman pursuing an advanced degree and choosing a path for her life yet still being told that ultimately, without ethnic connection, she deserves pity for not being somebody. The hosting friend finds himself in an embarrassing, if predictable, situation when his family heritage and academic world collide. For the Ital-ian grandmother, the specific origin did not matter as much as the ability to claim membership in one, any, ethnic group. Professional achievement held little importance in light of this shortcoming.

As Agresto relates this tale, the moment was uncomfortable, but he understood what his grandmother meant. She was not trying

52. Ibid., 135.
53. John Agresto, "What Grandma Knew," in *Beyond the Godfather*, 150.

to insult the young woman, but only expressing her genuine reaction to the woman's answer. He, too, appreciates the distinguishing character of an ethnic identity. He writes, "Beyond the silly and superficial habit we have of reducing ethnicity to food, heritage adds interest, charm, and above all, diversity of outlook, talents, and ways of life to country and depth and relation to our private lives. Like religion, ethnicity helps form our character and shape our horizons."[54] Even if firmly established in an educated elite, those who grew up in ethnic Catholic communities perceive the long-lasting influence that results from those surroundings. It is a membership that continues to define them no matter how far they travel from the old neighborhood.

The old neighborhoods are changing, though. While immigration and ethnic clashes might still affect parish life, the terms have changed. My children are more likely to participate in Catholic masses in the Spanish language than to hear of tension between Irish clergy and Italian laity. A growing Hispanic population and shrinking priesthood have resulted in the combining of parishes that blend cultural communities. When St. Charles Borromeo Church in Bensalem, on the outskirts of Philadelphia, merged with the largely Latino Our Lady of Fatima, for example, parishioners had to adjust to new circumstances. The shift has created challenges for members of both churches, and their pastor is trying to figure out how to minister to everyone as a united community. He has his work cut out for him.[55] Perhaps in several decades this will be the story of cultural Catholicism—a new immigrant tale of religious practice on American soil. In the meantime, ethnic Catholics with European roots conjure a mid-century church that determined neighborhood life.

54. Ibid., 151.

55. Catherine E. Soichet, "The Face of Our Church Is Changing," CNN, September 15, 2015, http://www.cnn.com/2015/09/12/us/catholic-church-demographic-changes-bensalem/index.html, accessed September 16, 2015.

# Conclusion

Ash Wednesday was always a dreaded day during my grade-school years. Not only did it begin the somber season of Lent and the obligatory forty-day fast, but it required the annual anguish of dealing with the ashes themselves. It started with the fate of one's seat on a particular side of the church as we processed in for our school Mass. If you found yourself in Msgr. O'Brien's line you were doomed for a large, distinctive cross on the forehead. He was notoriously heavy-handed. (When he retired, my priest-uncle Msgr. Purcell replaced him as pastor and, fortunately, had a lighter touch with the ashes.) If, by chance, you lucked out on Fr. Duggan's side you had a much better shot at a small smudge of a cross. Concern heightened as you sat in the pew and watched the newly ashed students return to their seats before your turn to walk down the aisle: you witnessed what your forehead had in store for the day. Then there was the moment of waiting in line, hoping against hope, that yours would be the second or third cross after the thumb's dip into the ashes; a fresh dip for your cross was the worst-case scenario. For girls, especially, one's hairstyle came into play. Those with bangs held a clear advantage. Still, everyone faced the worry of inadvertently scratching one's forehead and removing part of the sacramental blessing. While we may have been tempted to brush away the unattractive symbol of our mortality, we knew such action could get us in trouble with God, or worse, the sisters. The only good news, which we would not have even realized at the time, was that just about anyone we would see during the day would also have the Catholic symbol on their foreheads or at least understand the source of the black mark. Our young insecurities were unfounded, but how could we know any better? This was our world.

My children have not yet received ashes, a voluntary sacramental distributed once a year in the church's calendar. When they do, they will encounter something different. They might someday experience a nervous anticipation of Ash Wednesday, but they will not be surrounded by pews full of classmates, nor will they have confidence in the priest's ash-giving habits when they do. More likely than not, they will be at the mercy of a visiting priest or a lay minister. They will need to find time for the ritual around their public school-day schedule instead of the break in a Catholic school-day as I had. They might have to explain the smudge on their foreheads to people they meet, even in our Philadelphia suburb. Perhaps, though, they will find comfort through online social media where galleries of pictures show Catholics from places near and far donning their ashes. Instead of comparing their own ashen crosses to their classmates', they can check out some in Houston or Honduras or Hungary on a screen.

The origin and importance of ashes—the ones my parents received, those I remember, and the ones my children can anticipate—remain the same. A biblical sign of mourning as well as a reminder of our mortality and need for God, symbolic ashes call Catholics to repent as they begin the season of Lent. What has changed dramatically across generations, though, are the circumstances surrounding the annual rite. It is the same faith, but it is a different church.

This book has provided a window onto one generation's experience of this changing church. The variety of voices that depict mid-twentieth-century Catholicism in memoir and fiction allows readers to perceive the powerful and pervasive religious influence that determined much of everyday life for these Americans. Though it cannot claim a comprehensive history of Catholic life during the time, this assemblage of descriptions reveals a shared experience that might resonate for many.

As American Catholic generations move further away from an immigrant status that created ethnic enclaves; as dependence on the local parish for identity or community dissipates; as the world itself becomes ever-more accessible with the click of a button, the insular embrace of Catholic life that characterizes these mid-twentieth-century narrated experiences fades deeper into a collective memory. Likewise, my children's generation will form its own collective memories. Unlike their grandparents, who might have prayed for the conversion of souls in a far-away Africa at the family dinner table, the emerging cohorts might interact with visiting African Catholics at their local Sunday Mass. They might never use their parish's name to communicate who they are and where they are from, but they might convince a friend from across town to attend their youth ministry's Friday night disco bingo. They will remember the sound of church bells and the sight of stained glass on Sundays, but those memories might blend with the buzz of inadvertent cell phone rings or the image of our pastor delivering his homily from notes on his iPad. The details have changed.

My parents were shaped by the Catholicism that enveloped them at a particular time and in a particular place. Time will tell how my children will perceive and respond to the Catholicism they experience. Despite the vast difference between their everyday particulars, I take heart that their shared faith tradition connects them across generations.

# BIBLIOGRAPHY

Agresto, John. "What Grandma Knew." In *Beyond the Godfather: Italian American Writers on the Real Italian American Experience*, edited by A. Kenneth Ciongoli and Jay Parini, 150–52. Hanover, N.H.: University Press of New England, 1997.

Anderson, Karen. *Changing Woman: A History of Racial Ethnic Women in Modern America*. New York: Oxford University Press, 1996.

Appleby, R. Scott, and Kathleen Sprows Cummings. *Catholics in the American Century: Recasting Narratives of U.S. History*. Ithaca, N.Y.: Cornell University Press, 2012.

Ardizzone, Tony. "Baseball Fever." In *Taking It Home: Stories from the Neighborhood*, 1–18. Urbana: University of Illinois Press, 1996.

Avella, Steven M., and Elizabeth McKeown. *Public Voices: Catholics in the American Context*. Maryknoll, N.Y.: Orbis, 1999.

Baggett, Jerome P. *Sense of the Faithful*. Oxford: Oxford University Press, 2009.

Barolini, Helen. *Chiaroscuro: Essays of Identity*. Madison: University of Wisconsin Press, 1999.

Barry, Dan. *Pull Me Up: A Memoir*. New York: W. W. Norton, 2004.

Bayor, Ronald H. *Neighbors in Conflict: The Irish, Germans, Jews, and Italians of New York City, 1929–1941*. Baltimore: Johns Hopkins University Press, 1978.

*The Bells of St. Mary's*. Directed by Leo McCarey. 1945.

Blais, Madeleine. *Uphill Walkers: Memoir of a Family*. New York: Atlantic Monthly Press, 2001.

Bodo, Murray, OFM. "Holy Orders." In *Signatures of Grace: Writers on the Sacraments*, edited by Thomas Grady and Paula Huston, 164–92. New York: Dutton, 2000.

Brazile, Donna. *Cooking with Grease: Stirring the Pots in American Politics*. New York: Simon and Schuster, 2004.

Bryk, Anthony S., Valerie E. Lee, and Peter Blakely Holland. *Catholic Schools and the Common Good*. Cambridge, Mass.: Harvard University Press, 1993.

Buetow, Harold A. *Of Singular Benefit: The Story of Catholic Education in the United States*. New York: Macmillan, 1970.

Burns, Jeffrey M., Ellen Skerrett, and Joseph M. White, eds. *Keeping Faith: European and Asian Catholic Immigrants*. American Catholic Identities: A Documentary History. Maryknoll, N.Y.: Orbis, 2000.

Carey, Patrick. *Catholics in America: A History*. Lanham, Md.: Rowman and Littlefield, 2008.

Cascone, Gina. *Pagan Babies and Other Catholic Memories*. New York: St. Martin's Press, 1982.

"Catholics in America." *National Catholic Reporter*. October 24, 2011. https://www.ncronline.org/AmericanCatholics. Accessed July 18, 2016.

Chinnici, Joseph. "The Catholic Community at Prayer: 1926–1976." In *Habits of Devotion: Catholic Religious Practices of Twentieth Century America*, edited by James O'Toole, 9–88. Ithaca, N.Y.: Cornell University Press, 2004.

Ciresi, Rita. *Pink Slip*. New York: Delacorte, 1999.

——. "The Little Ice Age." In *Sometimes I Dream in Italian*, 120–51. New York: Dell, 2000.

Clinton, Kate. *Don't Get Me Started*. New York: Ballantine, 1998.

Cokal, Susan. "Immaculate Heart." In *Resurrecting Grace: Remembering Catholic Childhoods*, edited by Marilyn Sewell, 142–47. Boston: Beacon, 2001.

Congar, Yves. *Lay People in the Church*. Westminster, Md.: Newman Press, 1965.

Copeland, M. Shawn, ed. *Uncommon Faithfulness: The Black Catholic Experience*. Maryknoll, N.Y.: Orbis, 2009.

Corcoran, Sister M. Jerome. *The Catholic Elementary School Principal*. Milwaukee: Bruce, 1961.

Costello, Carol. "Pope Francis, Women Are Waiting." *CNN*. September 11, 2015. http://www.cnn.com/2015/09/10/opinions/costello-women-in-church/index.html. Accessed July 27, 2016.

Cummings, Kathleen Sprows. *New Women of the Old Faith: Gender and American Catholicism in the Progressive Era*. Chapel Hill: University of North Carolina Press, 2009.

D'Antonio, William, James Davidson, Mary Gautier, and Katherine Meyer. "Assumptions in Study on Young Catholics Lead to Unnecessarily Grim Outlook." *National Catholic Reporter*. December 6, 2014. https://www.ncronline.org/news/people/assumptions-study-young-catholics-lead-unnecessarily-grim-outlook. Accessed July 19, 2016.

D'Antonio, William, Michelle Dillon, and Mary L. Gautier. *American Catholics in Transition*. Lanham, Md.: Rowman and Littlefield, 2013.

Davis, Cyprian. *The History of Black Catholics in the United States*. New York: Crossroad, 1990.

DeMonte, Claudia. "The Whole World Was Italian." In *Growing Up Italian: How Being Brought Up as an Italian-American Helped Shape the Characters, Lives and Fortunes of Twenty-Four Celebrated Americans*, edited by Linda Brandi Cateura, 51–64. New York: William and Morrow, 1987.

Dolan, Jay P. *The American Catholic Experience: A History from Colonial Times to the Present*. Garden City, N.Y.: Doubleday, 1985.

———. *The American Catholic Parish: A History from 1850 to the Present*. 2 vols. New York: Paulist Press, 1987.

———. *The Immigrant Church: New York's Irish and German Catholics, 1815–1865*. Notre Dame, Ind.: University of Notre Dame Press, 1992.

———. *In Search of an American Catholicism: A History of Religion and Culture in Tension*. Oxford and New York: Oxford University Press, 2002.

Douglas, Jean K. *Why I Left the Church, Why I Came Back, and Why I Just Might Leave Again: Memories of Growing Up African American and Catholic*. Astor, Fla.: Fortuity, 2006.

Ferraro, Thomas. "Not-Just-Cultural Catholics." In *Catholic Lives, Contemporary America*, edited by Thomas Ferraro, 1–18. Durham, N.C.: Duke University Press, 1997.

———. *Feeling Italian: The Art of Ethnicity in America*. New York: New York University Press, 2005.

Fisher, James T. *Communion of Immigrants: A History of Catholics in America*. Oxford: Oxford University Press, 2002.

Flock, Elizabeth. "Generation X Becoming Less Catholic and Less Republican." *U.S. News and World Report*. May 31, 2012. http://www.usnews.com/news/articles/2012/05/31/generation-x-becoming-less-catholic-and-less-republican-. Accessed July 19, 2016.

Gambone, Philip. "Searching for Real Words." In *Wrestling with the Angel: Faith and Religion in the Lives of Gay Men*, edited by Brian Bouldrey, 221–42. New York: Riverhead, 1995.

Gamm, Gerald. *Urban Exodus: Why the Jews Left Boston and the Catholics Stayed*. Cambridge, Mass.: Harvard University Press, 1999.

Garcia, Mario T. *Católicos: Resistance and Affirmation in Chicano Catholic History*. Austin: University of Texas Press, 2008.

Gaudiani, Claire. "Of Cheese and Choices." In *Beyond the Godfather: Italian American Writers on the Real Italian American Experience*, edited by A. Kenneth Ciongoli and Jay Parini, 114–25. Hanover, N.H.: University Press of New England, 1997.

Gildiner, Catherine. *Too Close to the Falls: A Memoir*. New York: Viking, 1999.

Gilmour, Peter. "Spiritual Shifts (Odds and Ends)." *U.S. Catholic Magazine* 67, no. 1 (2002).

*Going My Way*. Directed by Leo McCarey. 1944.

Giuliani, Rudolph. "Outspoken Mayor, Battling Prosecutor." In *Growing Up Italian: Memoirs of Twenty-Four Celebrated Italian-Americans*, edited by Linda Brandi Catuera, 227–43. New York: William and Morrow Company, 1987.

Goodwin, Doris Kearns. "The Brooklyn Dodgers and the Catholic Church." In *I Like Being Catholic*, edited by Michael Leach and Therese J. Borchard, 67–69. New York: Doubleday, 2000.

Gordon, Mary. *Men and Angels*. Large print ed. Boston: G. K. Hall, 1986.

———. *Good Boys and Dead Girls: And Other Essays*. New York: Viking, 1991.

———. *Seeing through Places: Reflections on Geography and Identity*. New York: Scribner, 2000.

———. *Conversations with Mary Gordon*. Edited by Alma Bennett. Literary Conversations Series. Jackson: University Press of Mississippi, 2002.

———. "Women of God." *Atlantic*, January 2002. http://www.theatlantic.com/magazine/archive/2002/01/women-of-god/302377/. Accessed January 14, 2015.

———. "Temporary Shelter." In *The Stories of Mary Gordon*, 256–96. New York: Pantheon, 2006.

Gray, Mark M. "Your Average American Catholic." *America: National Catholic Review*. May 18, 2015. http://americamagazine.org/issue/your-average-american-catholic. Accessed July 19, 2016.

Greeley, Andrew M. *The Communal Catholic: A Personal Manifesto*. New York: Seabury, 1976.

———. *The Catholic Imagination*. Berkeley: University of California Press, 2000.

———. *The Catholic Revolution: New Wine, Old Wineskins and the Second Vatican Council*. Berkeley: University of California Press, 2004.

Grogan, John. *The Longest Trip Home: A Memoir*. New York: Harper, 2008.

Hall, David D. *Lived Religion in America: Toward a History of Practice*. Princeton: Princeton University Press, 1997.

Hampl, Patricia. *Virgin Time: In Search of the Contemplative Life*. New York: Ballantine, 1993.

———. "Penance." In *Signatures of Grace: Catholic Writers on the Sacraments*, edited by Thomas Grady and Paula Huston, 34–68. New York: Dutton, 2000.

———. *The Florist's Daughter*. Orlando, Fla.: Harcourt, 2007.

Hannan, James. "A Mixed Marriage." *Commonweal*. December 10, 2014. https://www.commonwealmagazine.org/blog/mixed-marriage. Accessed July 19, 2016.

Hansen, Ron. "Eucharist." In *Signatures of Grace: Catholics Writers on the Sacraments*, edited by Thomas Grady and Paula Huston, 69–97. New York: Dutton, 2000.

Hayes, Charlotte. "Catholic Identity and the Core Curriculum at Notre Dame." *National Catholic Register*. January 1, 2015. http://www.ncregister.com/daily-news/catholic-identity-and-the-core-curriculum-at-notre-dame/. Accessed July 19, 2016.

Herberg, Will. *Protestant Catholic Jew: An Essay in American Religious Sociology*. Chicago: University of Chicago Press, 1955.

Hoffert, Sylvia D. *A History of Gender in America: Essays, Documents, and Articles*. Upper Saddle River, N.J.: Prentice Hall, 2003.

Horowitz, Daniel. *Betty Friedan and the Making of the Feminine Mystique: The American Left, the Cold War, and Modern Feminism*. Amherst: University of Massachusetts, 1998.

Hunt, Thomas. "Historical Overview of Catholic Schools in the United States." In *Catholic Schools in the United States: An Encyclopedia*, edited by Thomas Hunt, Ellis A. Joseph, and Ronald J. Nuzzi. Westport, Conn.: Greenwood, 2004.

Irvine, Jacqueline Jordan, and Michele Foster, eds. *Growing Up African American in Catholic Schools*. New York: Teachers College Press, 1996.

Jabbar, Kareem Abdul, and Peter Knobler. *Giant Steps: The Autobiography of Kareem Abdul Jabbar*. New York: Bantam, 1983.

Kane, Paula. "Marian Devotion since 1940: Continuity or Casualty?" In *Habits of Devotion: Catholic Religious Practice in Twentieth-Century America*, edited by James M. O'Toole, 89–130. Cushwa Center Studies of Catholicism in Twentieth-Century America. Ithaca, N.Y.: Cornell University Press, 2004.

Katkin, Wendy F., Ned C. Landsman, and Andrea Tyree. *Beyond Pluralism: The Conception of Groups and Group Identities in America*. Urbana: University of Illinois Press, 1998.

Kivisto, Peter. *Incorporating Diversity: Rethinking Assimilation in a Multicultural Age*. Boulder, Colo.: Paradigm, 2005.

Kivisto, Peter, Dag Blanck, and Swenson Swedish Immigration Center. *American Immigrants and Their Generations: Studies and Commentaries on the Hansen Thesis after Fifty Years*. Urbana: University of Illinois Press, 1990.

Lane, Belden. "Giving Voice to Place: Three Models for Understanding Sacred Space." *Religion and American Culture* 11, no. 1 (2001): 53–81.

Laurino, Maria. *Were You Always an Italian?: Ancestors and Other Icons of Italian America*. New York: W. W. Norton, 2000.

Linden-Ward, Blanche, and Carol Hurd Green. *American Women in the 1960s: Changing the Future*. New York: Twayne, 1993.

Liptak, Dolores. *Immigrants and Their Church*. New York: Macmillan, 1989.

Malloy, Edward A. *Monk's Tale: The Pilgrimage Begins, 1941–1975*. Notre Dame, Ind.: University of Notre Dame Press, 2009.

Manning, Martha. *Chasing Grace: Reflections of a Catholic Girl, Grown Up*. San Francisco: HarperSanFrancisco, 1996.

Marty, Martin. "Religion: A Private Affair, in Public Affairs." *Religion and American Culture* 3, no. 2 (1993).

Mason, Alane Salierno. "The Exegesis of Eating." In *The Milk of Almonds: Italian American -Women Writers on Food and Culture*, edited by Louise DeSalvo and Edvige Giunta, 261–68. New York: Feminist Press at CUNY, 2002.

Massa, Mark. *Catholics and American Culture: Fulton Sheen, Dorothy Day, and the Notre Dame Football Team*. New York: Crossroad, 1999.

Massa, Mark, and Catherine Osborne. *American Catholic History: A Documentary Reader*. New York: New York University Press, 2008.

Matovina, Timothy M. *Latino Catholicism: Transformation in America's Largest Church*. Princeton: Princeton University Press, 2011.

Matovina, Timothy M., and Gary Riebe-Estrella, eds. *Horizons of the Sacred: Mexican Traditions in U.S. Catholicism*. Ithaca, N.Y.: Cornell University Press, 2002.

McAvoy, Thomas Timothy. *The Americanist Heresy in Roman Catholicism: 1895–1900*. Notre Dame, Ind.: University of Notre Dame Press, 1963.

McCartin, James P. *Prayers of the Faithful: The Shifting Spiritual Life of American Catholics*. Cambridge, Mass.: Harvard University Press, 2010.

McDannell, Colleen. *Material Christianity: Religion and Popular Culture in America*. New Haven, Conn.: Yale University Press, 1995.

———. *The Spirit of Vatican II: A History of Catholic Reform in America*. New York: Basic Books, 2011.

McDermott, Alice. *A Bigamist's Daughter: A Novel*. New York: Random House, 1982.

———. "Confessions of a Reluctant Catholic: Portrait of a Novelist." *Commonweal*, February 11, 2000: 12–16.

———. *Child of My Heart*. New York: Farrar, Straus and Giroux, 2002.

———. "Lunatic in the Pew." In *The Best Catholic Writing 2004*, edited by Brian Doyle, 1–10. Chicago: Loyola Press, 2004.

McDermott, Jim. "It's Commencement Controversy Season!" *America: National Catholic Review*. May 5, 2016. http://americamagazine.org/content/dispatches/its-commencement-controversy-season. Accessed July 19, 2016.

McGreevy, John T. *Parish Boundaries: The Catholic Encounter with Race in the Twentieth Century Urban North*. Chicago: University of Chicago Press, 1996.

———. *Catholicism and American Freedom: A History*. New York: W. W. Norton, 2003.

McGuire, Michael A. *Father McGuire's the New Baltimore Catechism*. New York: Benziger Brothers, 1942.

Milhaven, Annie Lally. "Mary Gordon." Interview. In *Conversations with Mary Gordon*, edited by Alma Bennett, 42–56. Jackson: University of Mississippi Press, 2002.

Moore, Edmund Arthur. *A Catholic Runs for President: The Campaign of 1928.* New York: Ronald, 1956.

Morgan, David. *Visual Piety: A History and Theory of Popular Religious Images.* Berkeley: University of California Press, 1998.

Morris, Charles R. *American Catholic: The Saints and Sinners Who Built America's Most Powerful Church.* New York: Times Books, 1997.

Morrow, Maria C. *Sin the in the Sixties: Catholics and Confession 1955–1965.* Washington, D.C.: The Catholic University of America Press, 2016.

Moses, Paul. *An Unlikely Union: The Love-Hate Story of New York's Irish and Italians.* New York: New York University Press, 2015.

Mugavero, Bishop Francis J. "Italian among the Irish." In *Growing Up Italian: Memoirs of Twenty-Four Celebrated Italian-Americans*, edited by Linda Brandi Catuera. 97–106. New York: William and Morrow, 1987.

Nabhan-Warren, Kristy. "Hispanics and Religion in America." *Oxford Research Encyclopedia of Religion.* March 2016. http://religion.oxfordre.com/view/10.1093/acrefore/9780199340378.001.0001/acrefore-9780199340378-e-79. Accessed January 6, 2017.

*The Nun's Story.* Directed by Fred Zinnemann. 1959.

O'Connor, Richard. *The First Hurrah: A Biography of Alfred E. Smith.* New York: Putnam, 1970.

Olson, James Stuart. *Catholic Immigrants in America.* Chicago: Nelson Hall, 1987.

Orsi, Robert A. *The Madonna of 115th Street: Faith and Community in Italian Harlem, 1880–1950.* New Haven, Conn.: Yale University Press, 1985.

———. *Between Heaven And Earth: The Religious Worlds People Make and the Scholars Who Study Them.* Princeton: Princeton University Press, 2005.

O'Toole, James M. "'The Newer Catholic Races': The Varieties of Ethnic Catholicism." In *Militant and Triumphant: William Henry O'Connell and the Catholic Church of Boston, 1859–1944.* Notre Dame, Ind.: University of Notre Dame Press, 1992.

———, ed. *Habits of Devotion: Catholic Religious Practice in Twentieth-Century America.* Cushwa Center Studies of Catholicism in Twentieth-Century America. Ithaca, N.Y.: Cornell University Press, 2004.

———. "In the Court of Conscience: American Catholics and Confession, 1900–1975." In *Habits of Devotion: Catholic Religious Devotion in Twentieth-Century America.* Ithaca, N.Y.: Cornell University Press, 2004.

———. *The Faithful: A History of Catholics in America.* Cambridge, Mass.: Belknap Press of Harvard University Press, 2008.

Parini, Jay. "Amalfi Days." In *Beyond the Godfather: Italian American Writers on the Real Italian American Experience*, edited by Jay Parini and A. Kenneth Ciongoli, 107–13. Hanover, N.H.: University Press of New England, 1997.

Paulson, Michael. "Even As Hispanics Lift Catholicism, Many Are Leaving the Church." *New York Times*. May 7, 2014. http://www.nytimes.com/2014/05/08/upshot/even-as-hispanics-lift-catholicism-theyre-leaving-it.html?_r=0. Accessed July 19, 2016.

Peyton, Father Patrick, CSC. *The Rosary Priest*. n.d. http://www.fatherpeyton.org. Accessed February 3, 2016.

Plante, David. *American Ghosts*. Boston: Beacon, 2005.

———. *The Catholic*. New York: Atheneum, 1986.

Portier, W. L., N. Dallavalle, C. C. Roberts, T. Beattie, R. R. Reno, P. Hampl . . . P. Baumann. "A Modus Vivendi: Sex, Marriage and the Church." *Commonweal*. December 27, 2011. https://www.commonwealmagazine.org/modus-vivendi. Accessed July 19, 2016.

Quindlen, Anna. *Living Out Loud*. New York: Ballantine, 1994.

———. *Object Lessons*. New York: Fawcett, 1991.

———. *How Reading Changed My Life*. Library of Contemporary Thought. New York: Ballantine, 1998.

Ramirez, Bishop Ricardo. *Power from the Margins: The Emergence of the Latino in the Church and in Society*. Maryknoll, N.Y.: Orbis, 2016.

Rangel, Charles B., with Leon Wynter. *And I Haven't Had a Bad Day Since: From the Streets of Harlem to the Halls of Congress*. New York: Thomas Dunne, 2007.

Rice, Anne. *Called Out of Darkness: A Spiritual Confession*. New York: Anchor, 2008.

Rivera, Edward. *Family Installments: Memories of Growing Up Hispanic*. New York: Penguin, 1983.

Rodriguez, Richard. *Hunger of Memory: The Education of Richard Rodriguez; An Autobiography*. Boston: D. R. Godine, 1982.

———. *Days of Obligation: An Argument with My Mexican Father*. New York: Viking, 1992.

———. "The Fabric of Our Identity." Interview by Krista Tippett. *On Being*. Podcast. September 18, 2014.

Rosenwald, Michael S., and Michelle Boorstein. "Denying Communion: A Priest and a Lesbian Set off a Catholic Culture Clash." *Washington Post*. March 17, 2012. https://www.washingtonpost.com/local/denying-communion-a-priest-and-a-lesbian-set-off-a-catholic-culture-clash/2012/03/15/gIQA9roNJS_story.html. Accessed July 19, 2016.

Ruane, John Bernard. *Parish the Thought: An Inspirational Memoir of Growing Up Catholic in the 1960s*. Roswell, Ga.: Roswell Press, 2007.

Rumbaut, Rubén, and Alejandro Portes, eds. *Ethnicities: Children of Immigrants in America*. Berkeley: University of California Press, 2001.

Sandoval, Moises. *On the Move: A History of the Hispanic Church in the United States.* 2nd ed. Maryknoll, N.Y.: Orbis, 2006.

Santiago, Esmeralda. *When I Was Puerto Rican.* New York: Vintage, 1994.

Schmalz, Valerie. "University President Defends Hiring for Catholic Identity." *American Catholic.* July 13, 2016. http://www.americancatholic.org/news/report.aspx?id=44844. Accessed July 19, 2016.

Schneible, Ann. "Women Are Irreplaceable for Passing on the Faith, Pope says." *Catholic News Agency.* January 26, 2015. http://www.catholicnewsagency.com/news/women-are-irreplaceable-in-passing-on-the-faith-pope-says-21135/. Accessed July 27, 2016.

Scott, Joan W. "Gender: A Useful Category of Cultural Analysis." *American Historical Review* 91, no. 5 (1986): 1053–175.

Smith, Anthony Burke. *The Look of Catholics: Portrayals in Popular Culture from the Great Depression to the Cold War.* Lawrence: University Press of Kansas, 210.

Smith, Tom. *Transcript of the Book Show* (1992). New York State Writers Institute. 1998. http://www.albany.edu/writers-inst/olv2n3.html#mcdermott. Accessed March 4, 2006.

Soichet, Catherine E. "The Face of Our Church Is Changing." CNN. September 12, 2015. http://www.cnn.com/2015/09/12/us/catholic-church-demographic-changes-bensalem/index.html. Accessed September 14, 2015.

Sollors, Werner. *The Invention of Ethnicity.* New York: Oxford University Press, 1988.

——. *Theories of Ethnicity: A Classical Reader.* New York: New York University Press, 1996.

*The Song of Bernadette.* Directed by Henry King. 1943.

Sotomayor, Sonia. *My Beloved World.* New York: Alfred A. Knopf, 2013.

Stivender, Ed. *Raised Catholic: Can You Tell?* Little Rock: August House, 1992.

Sullivan, Amy. "Does Biden Have a Catholic Problem?" *Time.* September 13, 2008. http://content.time.com/time/politics/article/0,8599,1840965,00.html. Accessed July 19, 2016.

Tardy, Jo Anne. *A Light Will Rise in the Darkness: Growing Up Black and Catholic in New Orleans.* Skokie, Ill.: ACTA, 2006.

Tentler, Leslie Woodcock. *Catholics and Contraception: An American History.* Ithaca, N.Y.: Cornell University Press, 2004.

Torgovnick, Marianna De Marco. *Crossing Ocean Parkway.* Chicago: University of Chicago Press, 1994.

Traub, George W., ed. *A Jesuit Education Reader.* Chicago: Loyola Press, 2008.

Van Beeck, Frans Jozef. "Denying Communion to Politicians: A Theologian Explains Why It's Wrong." *Commonweal.* June 14, 2004. https://www

.commonwealmagazine.org/denying-communion-politicians-0. Accessed July 19, 2016.

Wachtel, Eleanor. "Mary Gordon." Interview. In *Conversations with Mary Gordon*, edited by Alma Bennett, 81–89. Jackson: University of Mississippi Press, 2002.

Wandersee, Winifred D. *On the Move: American Women in the 1970s*. Boston: Twayne, 1988.

Ward, Leo R. "Principles for Principals." In *The Catholic Elementary School Principal*, by Sister M. Jerome Corcoran. Milwaukee: Bruce, 1961.

Waters, Mary C. *Ethnic Options: Choosing Identities in America*. Berkeley: University of California Press, 1990.

White, C. Vanessa. "Authentically Black and Truly Catholic." September 5, 2010. http://www.cnn.com/2010/OPINION/09/05/white.catholic.black/index.html. Accessed July 7, 2016.

White, Deborah G. *Too Heavy a Load: Black Women in Defense of Themselves 1894–1994*. New York: W. W. Norton, 1999.

Wilcox, John R., and Irene King. *Enhancing Religious Identity: Best Practices from Catholic Campuses*. Washington D.C.: Georgetown University Press, 2000.

Wills, Garry. *Why I Am a Catholic*. Boston: Houghton Mifflin, 2002.

———. *Bare Ruined Choirs: Doubt, Prophecy, and Radical Religion*. New York: Paulist Press, 2014.

———. "Memories of a Catholic Boyhood." In *Bare Ruined Choirs: Doubt, Prophesy and Radical Religion*, 17–41. New York: Paulist Press, 2014.

Wood, Monica. *When We Were the Kennedys: A Memoir from Mexico, Maine*. New York: Houghton Mifflin, 2012.

*World Meeting of Families Icon*. 2015. http://www.worldmeeting2015.org/about-the-event/icon/. Accessed February 2016.

*World Meeting of Families Prayer*. 2015. http://www.worldmeeting2015.org/about-the-event/prayer/. Accessed February 2016.

Youniss, James, and John J. Convey. *Catholic Schools at the Crossroads: Survival and Transformation*. New York: Teachers College Press, 2000.

Youniss, James, John J. Convey, and Jeffrey A. McLellan. *The Catholic Character of Catholic Schools*. Notre Dame, Ind.: University of Notre Dame Press, 2000.

# INDEX

perception as a threat, 141; ethnic background and advanced education, 142–43; formation of Christians and, 22; Irish Catholics' view of, 32; Italian Catholics' view of, 140–41; opportunities afforded by, 140–41; perception of bias against Catholics in higher education, 141. *See also* parochial schools

ethnic Catholicism: advanced education and, 142–43; allegiance to ethnic affiliations within Catholicism, 124–25; centrality of parish to neighborhood life, 19–20, 29–30, 116, 119–20; changes due to growing Hispanic population, 143; elders' perception of threat from education, 141; geography and demography of neighborhoods and, 117–22; judgments based on ethnicity, 122–23; neighborhoods facilitating a connection to religious heritage, 116; opportunities afforded by education, 140–41; racism within American Catholicism, 125; reaction to election of a Catholic president, 141–42; social hierarchies within parish, 138–39; tension among ethnic Catholics, 30–32; transparency of ethnic heritages, 123. *See also* Irish Catholics; Italian Catholics

ethnic neighborhoods. *See* Catholic neighborhoods

*Faithful, The* (O'Toole), 6, 7

family religious life. *See* religion in the home

*Feeling Italian* (Ferraro), 135

*Feminine Mystique, The* (Friedan), 93

Ferraro, Thomas, 4, 135

First Holy Communion: discipline in sacramental preparation, 54–55; preparation and thought required for, 65–66; range of children's depth of understanding of, 71–73; significance of, 70–71

Francis, Pope, 14, 111

Friedan, Betty, 93

Gambone, Philip, 103–5

Gaudiani, Claire, 96, 135

Gautier, Mary L., xv

German Catholics, 122

Gildiner, Catherine, 39–40, 95

Gilmour, Peter, 67

"Girl Child in a Women's World" (Gordon), 123

Giuliani, Rudolph, 134

*Going My Way* (movie), 130

Goodwin, Doris Kearns, 18

Gordon, Mary, 10, 32; on aura of a nun, 37–39; characteristics of the Catholic world, 62–63; on elders' perception of education, 141; on expected commitment to motherhood, 92; experiences in confessional, 67; family religious rituals, 80–81; impression left by displayed religious images, 88; on inherited Catholicism, 112–13; on insular nature of Catholic neighborhoods, 29; on Irish propensity for guilt, 132–33; on laity's relationship to priests, 44–45; memories of her neighborhood, 117–18, 123; social hierarchies within parish, 138

Greely, Andrew, 5

Grogan, John, 20, 59

Guadiani, Claire, 82, 129

Hampl, Patricia, 10; on expected commitment to moral standards, 91–92; experiences in confessional, 69; on filial obligations, 109–10; lessons learned about acceptable sexual behavior, 99, 101; memories of her neighborhood, 118; on rituals in the church, 55–56; view of being Irish, 126

Hannan, James, 136–37

Hansen, Ron, 72–73

Hispanic Catholics, 32–33, 143

Holy Orders, 42, 43

home. *See* religion in the home

homosexuality, 102–5

"Immaculate Heart" (Cokal), 99–101

institutional church: assimilation of U.S. Catholics, 17–18, 26; attention to students' religious and moral adherence, 22–23; centrality of local church to structure of life, 19–20; devotional practices, 20–21; ethnic solidarity in

institutional church: (*cont.*)
parishes, 16–17; European immigrants to the United States and, 16; goal of integrating education with Christian formation, 22. *See also* parochial schools

Irish Catholics: attitudes toward education, 32; changes in generational experiences of, 137–38; characteristics of, 31, 122; claiming of Catholicism, 123–24; element of death in Irish-American Catholic practice, 131–32; fidelity to church traditions, 130–31, 134; influences on children's paths, 96; propensity for guilt and silence, 132–33; resentment/nostalgia spectrum, 126–28; roles and assumptions assigned to, 133; social hierarchies within parish, 139; tension with Italians, 30–32

Italian Catholics: attitudes toward education, 32; centrality of religion to identity, 108; changes in generational experiences, 137–38; characteristics of, 122; claiming of Catholicism, 123–24; devotion to saints, 134–35; influences on children's paths, 97; resentment/nostalgia spectrum, 128–29; significance of food and family to, 135–36; social hierarchies within parish, 139; tensions with the Irish, 30–32; view of education, 140–41

Jews, 122
John XXIII, Pope, xiv
John Paul II, Pope, 78

Kane, Paula, 28, 92
Kennedy, John F., 27, 141–42
kinship and Catholicism: centrality of religion to peoples' identity, 107–9; connection between Catholic practice and filial obligation, 109–10; inescapability of inherited Catholicism, 112–13; lifelong implications of family's Catholicism, 107–9; women's implicit responsibility for passing on religious heritage, 110–11
Ku Klux Klan, 26

LaFarge, John, 125
Latino/a Catholics, 32–33, 143
Laurino, Maria: on her ethnic neighborhood, 123; on Irish fidelity to the church, 134; prominence of religious objects in her family space, 86; on social hierarchies within parish, 138–39; on women as standard bearers of devotion, 91
Lent, 145–46
Lord's Prayer, 85
Lourdes, France, 94–95

Malloy, Edward A., 116
Manning, Martha: on expected commitment to Virgin Mary, 93; experiences in confessional, 66; on power held by nuns, 49; on praying for vocations, 40; on significance of attending wakes, 131; view of being Irish, 126
Markoe, William, 125
Massa, Mark, 29
McCartin, James P., 7
McDannell, Colleen, 7, 21
McDermott, Alice, 10; centrality of religion to family's identity, 107–8; environment of her home, 25; experiences in confessional, 69; father's contribution to family's religion, 97–98; fidelity to her faith, 111–12; memories of her Catholic neighborhood, 119; memories of structured school days, 52; on tenacity of being Catholic, 57–58, 76; view of being Irish, 127
McGreevy, John, 27, 119–20
*Men and Angels* (Gordon), 92
Morris, Charles, 19
Moses, Paul, 31
Mugavero, Bishop Francis G., 96–97

neighborhoods. *See* Catholic neighborhoods; ethnic Catholicism
nuns: aura of, 37–39; children's awareness of humanity of, 50, 51, 53–54; children's training to respect, 1–2; cultural impact of shrinking numbers of, 46; high standards established by, 39–40; impact of Vatican II on communities